The Charismatic Christian Church

Chris Legebow

ISBN- 978-1-988914-11-4

DEDICATION

This book is dedicated to those Apostles, Prophets, Pastors, Evangelists and Teachers who have impacted my life with the preaching of the gospel of Jesus Christ. Also, it is for those who are studying for ministry who truly give themselves wholly to God in Christian service.

CONTENTS

Chris Legebow

ACKNOWLEDGMENTS

All Scripture taken from Biblegateway.
MEV and KJV

FORWARD

Forward

This book on the Church contains Biblical history, and Church Doctrine. It is not meant to be the only viewpoint on the Church although the viewpoint expressed of the Church is presented as the Church as an ideal – God's ideal for Christians. It is a charismatic non-denominal perspective although certainly charismatic denominal churches can relate to it.

It is my hope you will recognize yourself in its pages and be able to communicate these things to others. Some of the topics seem so ordinary in excellent churches that they may not even recognize them as important. There are certain things mentioned that all successful churches are doing, but they may not realize the importance of them.

My book is a Biblical discussion of the Church with scripture as the main reference. The Church as the Body of Christ and Bride of Christ are discussed as well as the modern-day local church and its importance. This book is meant for those in ministry or those hoping to go into ministry. It is an evaluation of what the Church is and how the Church should be functioning in the earth. The reasons given are scriptural.

I've been a part of several successful charismatic churches but also volunteered ministry at some denominational churches. This book is a culmination of experience and training for ministry. It is the result of much prayer and Bible study.

Please take what you can from it and use as applicable. May God bless you in your pursuit of ministry.

Ephesians 1: — [6]to the praise of his glorious grace, which he has freely given us in the One he loves. [7]In him we have redemption through his blood, the forgiveness of sins, in accordance with the riches of God's grace [8]that he lavished on us. With all wisdom and understanding, [9]he[d] made known to us the mystery of his will according to his good pleasure, which he purposed in Christ, [10]to be put into effect when the times reach their fulfillment—to bring unity to all things in heaven and on earth under Christ.

Colossians 1: [26]the mystery that has been kept hidden for ages and generations, but is now disclosed to the Lord's people. [27]To them God has chosen to make known among the Gentiles the glorious riches of this mystery, which is Christ in you, the hope of glory.

[28]He is the one we proclaim, admonishing and teaching everyone with all wisdom, so that we may

present everyone fully mature in Christ. [29] To this end I strenuously contend with all the energy Christ so powerfully works in me.

1 The Church is the Body of Christ

The Body of Christ is the Church. The Church is referred to by different names in the Scripture. This chapter is about the Church as Jesus Christ's Body on the earth. We are His body on the earth. Jesus Christ lives in us and we who are Christians are His body. It doesn't mean that Jesus doesn't have a body. He is seated on the throne in His resurrected human body. The nail scars are in his hands and feet. Because He lives in our Spirit in the person of the Holy Spirit, we are as sacred consecrated body – each Christian is a temple of the Holy Spirit. The Holy presence of God lives in us, but we are also corporately the Body of Christ because we are His dwelling place. As we gather together, Jesus manifest's His glory in our midst.

Matthew 18: [19] "Again, truly I tell you that if two of you on earth agree about anything they ask for, it will be done for them by my Father in heaven. [20] For where two or three gather in my name, there am I with them."

The Holy Spirit in us, and through us is Christ's expression of love in the earth. Corporately, we have the title of the Universal Church – God's presence on the earth is in us. The first instance of the reference to the Church is the place we begin. Jesus was speaking with

His disciples on the earth while he was on the earth. He asked them "who do you say I am? "Because some people thought he was a prophet; some thought he was Elijah. Some thought He was a Teacher.

Peter answered him. Matthew 16: [16]Simon Peter answered, "You are the Messiah, the Son of the living God."

Jesus immediately spoke to Peter a word of exhortation. Jesus said on this rock I will build my Church.

Matthew 16: [17]Jesus replied, "Blessed are you, Simon son of Jonah, for this was not revealed to you by flesh and blood, but by my Father in heaven. [18]And I tell you that you are Peter,[b] and on this rock I will build my church, and the gates of Hades[c] will not overcome it.

"This rock" has been interpreted to mean Peter because Peter's name means rock. It is true that Peter was a very essential part of the church because he was one of the first 12 disciples and he lived his life preaching and teaching about Jesus, He was a foundation of the early Church and He died as a martyr for His faith. Although this is true, it is not the only meaning of "this rock" Jesus was referring to. Peter had a divine revelation of who Jesus was. Peter spoke by the inspiration of the Holy Spirit. Flesh and blood did not reveal it to him. It was not something he was taught. It is "this rock" of inspiration, divine revelation that Jesus is speaking about as the foundation of the Church. It is not simply words, but God's inspired words. The divine teacher who revealed it to Peter is the Holy Spirit. The Holy Spirit gave him the revelation and the utterance. It is the living presence of God in us that makes us different from any other religion. The Holy Spirit's presence in our lives inspires us to live as Christians, to speak, to minister to be the Body of Christ on the earth. The Holy Spirit gives us revelation, insight, wisdom, application of wisdom etc. God dwells in us.

1 Corinthians 12 is an excellent chapter to study the spiritual gifts of the Church. I emphasize it in other places but here I am going to emphasize a different part of it. The body of Christ is discussed in much detail. This is a sustained comparison or allegory – the Church and the human body are compared.

1 Corinthians 12: [12] Just as a body, though one, has many parts, but all its many parts form one body, so it is with Christ. [13] For we were all baptized by[c] one Spirit so as to form one body—whether Jews or Gentiles, slave or free—and we were all given the one Spirit to drink. [14] Even so the body is not made up of one part but of many.

This passage of scripture is saying we are like a body – a human body connected members all essential to the well being of the body. It talks about the different parts of the body of Christ. We are all joined together by the Spirit of God that dwells within us. We are joined because we were all baptized into Jesus Christ. The parts of the body are all very different but also essential to the well being of the body. There are no extra body parts.

1 Corinthians 12:[15] Now if the foot should say, "Because I am not a hand, I do not belong to the body," it would not for that reason stop being part of the body.[16] And if the ear should say, "Because I am not an eye, I do not belong to the body," it would not for that reason stop being part of the body.[17] If the whole body were an eye, where would the sense of hearing be? If the whole body were an ear, where would the sense of smell be? [18] But in fact God has placed the parts in the body, every one of them, just as he wanted them to be. [19] If they were all one part, where would the body be? [20] As it is, there are many parts, but one body.

Members of the Body of Christ

All the parts of your body are necessary. I've met people who might be missing a limb or a finger or toe because of some instance or by birth. They manage but it is not quite the same as having all your body parts. God can bless those who are missing a body part. They can excel by compensation. I am comparing the Church to a physical body. There are no extra parts on the human body and there are no extra parts in the body of Christ. Although we all function differently, all aspects are necessary for the body to preserve itself in homeostasis. We need all our fingers. They help us to grasp objects and do fine motor skills. We need our thumb. Our apposable thumb makes us different than all other creatures. Only humans have it. It means you can move your thumb back and forth. You can squeeze your thumb to your index finger. You can squeeze your thumb to your baby finger. You can rotate your thumb in a circular motion. It gives us a unique grasp. No other creature has it. I don't know if you have thought of how fascinating your own hand is but it is. By human will – instantly your body responds to your brain. I want to shake your hand – my arm lifts and my hand shoots out towards you. It is immediate.

Even if a chimpanzee was really smart, well taught, how to drive a stick shift car, he or she couldn't do it easily because only human's have the thumb that can grasp in a full ball joint. Take a moment to count approximately how often you use your hands in one hour. Each thing we do, we use our hands – picking things up, putting them down, writing, typing, carrying objects etc.

Without your eyes, what could you see? Your body would compensate but you would miss the gift of sight. Yet if we were all eyes, we couldn't function. We need our ears to communicate and to discern situations. There are no extra parts on a human body.

When a baby is young, he or she doesn't know how to use his or her body. He or she must develop motor skills and learn how to use them. New babies don't do much. They depend on the parents for everything. They just sort of lie there. The parents give the baby a bottle but must hold it or prop it up because the baby doesn't know how to hold it and can't coordinate his body to do it. Babies begin to move their limbs haphazardly and eventually with some skill so they can kick on purpose or wave their arms or hands on purpose.

Development

After a little while, the baby will learn how to put his hand around the baby bottle. He or she knows that it is necessary. Grasping the bottle is one of the first things he or she learns. Soon he or she develops strength in the muscles so he or she can support the bottle with both hands alone. The baby learns to crawl to move around. I don't know if you have seen a baby try to walk but I can remember myself learning to walk. I have a pretty vivid memory of my early childhood. I can remember I had a jumper swing. I would use my legs to propel myself, but the weight of my body was help up by the seat. I developed muscular strength in my legs from using it. I had a small cart with wheels on it and a baby seat. I would use my legs to move around but once more I was seated, and the weight of my body was held by the device. I could go in any direction but the easiest was to go forward. These little walkers allow the kid to stretch his or her legs while learning about movement, develop muscle strength. One cannot get those same things in Canada anymore because of stairs and other reasons, but you can still get them in the USA.

The point of my story is not so much to give you details of my cute childhood but to explain how muscles develop in the body. The baby has got all the parts of a body as an adult, but the baby doesn't know how to use his or body. He or she must learn. He or she must develop muscular strength. Muscular development must also be accompanied by teaching by the parents. Usually parents, in my instance it was my mum, my sister or my nanny. They would show me how to hold something. They played finger counting games with me. They would teach me to clap, to grasp, to throw etc. All of things, moving the fingers or the hands or the body, we take for granted as adults.

So is the Body of Christ. A new baby in Christ, is instantly saved. The person has got the Holy Spirit living on the inside of him or her with spiritual gifts and spiritual fruit buds. The gifts and the fruit, a mature Christian has are in essence in the new Christian but he or she must learn how to use each gift or talent. The only way for a baby Christian to develop is through being with other Christians to receive teaching as well as exercising and using his or her spiritual gifts. There is also the important aspect of having a relationship with God that quickens us and empowers us, inspires us, teaches us etc.

A prophet in the body of Christ is a visionary as well as a mouthpiece for God. The prophet learns how to use these spiritual gifts by practice and use. A prophet watches over the church as a watchman (Ez.33: 6) caring for the body and praying over it. They speak by inspiration of the Holy Spirit what God would have them speak to the Church. More detail is given in my teaching on Spiritual gifts.

Accepting Christ

A baby Christian is immediately part of the body of Christ. There are no Junior Christians or training Christians or apprentice Christians. As soon as you receive Christ, you became a Christian – you are a part of the body of Christ. There are no extra parts. On a bicycle there are training wheels to support a child learning to ride. Eventually, the child learns to ride a two-wheeler with balance. In some professions they have apprentices.

My dad was a carpenter. He often trained apprentices to help him in jobs, showing them how to use the equipment. Eventually they serve the senior carpenter until they fulfill their training and can function on their own as carpenters doing all aspects of the job. We don't have the same thing in the body of Christ – in becoming a Christian. Of course. a new Christian develops his Spiritual fruit and Spiritual gifts by studying alongside and serving with a mature Christian. I am emphasizing that a baby Christian is immediately part of the body of Christ. The person has been translated out of the kingdom of darkness into the kingdom of light. The Holy Spirit comes to live inside of the person. As soon as the spirit and the mouth confess Jesus as Saviour and LORD, the Holy Spirit comes to dwell within the person. The person is a part of the Body in particular (1 Cor 12: 27). There are no extra members. He or she is important, unique; God will manifest His or her glory through the person differently than anyone else.

Role in the body

It is important for us to learn our roll in the body of Christ. Because you are no extra. A new Christian can manifest spiritual gifts as soon as they become a Christian. With use and practice, he or she can develop those gifts. My own mother was not a Christian, she believed in Jesus – but she was in a cult not believing the divinity of Christ. She became a Christian and was baptized in the Holy Spirit the same day. It is a miracle – speaking in other tongues, because the Holy Spirit living in you gives you the utterance. This is especially true concerning my mother because she was adamant against it. She had many talks with me explaining to me that the gifts of the Holy Spirit are not for today and she was against it. She reprimanded me and would get angry speaking to me because I believed the literal Scripture that it is for all Christians.

Acts 2: [38] Peter replied, "Repent and be baptized, every one of you, in the name of Jesus Christ for the forgiveness of your sins. And you will receive the gift of the Holy Spirit. [39] The promise is for you and your children and for all who are far off—for all whom the Lord our God will call."

The Baptism of the Holy Spirit

The scripture says plainly it is for all Christians. It brought me so much joy that it was the first gift she manifested the same day she got saved. She knew that it was true because it happened to her. She knew it was God's Spirit. Also, she was moved on by the Holy Spirit right away. She wanted to pray for people. Immediately she felt prompted to go pray for people at the alter. She was just several days a Christian when she felt a burning in her hand and felt God wanted her to pray for people to be healed. She was a new Christian. No one taught her those things. She didn't believe in them in her other religion. She immediately felt it by the Spirit of God prompting her on the inner most being. Even as a baby Christian, she felt to use her spiritual gifts. A new Christian might prophesy. A new Christian might show mercy or compassion. A new Christian could use the gifts of the Spirit as they emerge but only by use and continual use in the Body of Christ are they developed fully.

Myself, as soon as I became a Christian, I began telling every person I knew about Christ. I started giving my testimony. One day a Christian, I didn't even know how to pray the sinner's prayer with someone, I thought it was words that you had to say that were scripted or something, I brought a friend to the person who lead me to Christ, so we could pray that prayer together. Even though I knew nothing about living as a Christian, I knew Jesus lived in me and that my life had been changed. My desire to share the truth with people was stronger than my ignorance of Christian lifestyle or functioning as a Christian. I knew nothing about being a Christian except what I learned from the Holy Spirit, the Scriptures and Christian people who invested in me.

When we lead people to Christ, we should inform them that they have Spiritual gifts and they should use them. They could contact us for any questions regarding their new life. I am so glad someone shared Christ with me. I immediately was changed. I was never the same. I began to perceive all the earth differently. The person also let me know that within me were spiritual gifts and that God would begin revealing them to me as I prayed and read the Bible and was in the church. I didn't know what it meant immediately, but I began to study the Bible immediately and God began to reveal to me through the Scriptures different aspects of my identity as a Christian.

Identifying with Christ

We must instruct new Christians in their identity as a Christian as well as their Spiritual gifts and talents and developing them. We must emphasize to the new Christians, they are Christians immediately. Should they die that day, they will go into the presence of God as sure as a saint who was older. The Holy Spirit will immediately begin prompting, leading, teaching, directing the new

Christian. It is comparable to that human baby that is learning to use his limbs and body parts except the Holy Spirit instructs us from within. Yes, it is essential to get mentored by mature Christians because a new Christian who was not raised in a Christian home has very different ideas than someone who has been taught the Scriptures from youth.

There are some common Spiritual gifts and callings we all have such as being ministers of reconciliation. We should all want to share what Christ has done for us with as many people as possible. As we are now ambassadors for Christ – parts of the body recruiting or evangelizing. You don't have to take an in-depth study class of evangelism before you can win somebody to Christ – you can do it as soon as you are saved.

2 Corinthians 5: [16]So from now on we regard no one from a worldly point of view. Though we once regarded Christ in this way, we do so no longer.[17]Therefore, if anyone is in Christ, the new creation has come:[a] The old has gone, the new is here! [18]All this is from God, who reconciled us to himself through Christ and gave us the ministry of reconciliation: [19]that God was reconciling the world to himself in Christ, not counting people's sins against them. And he has committed to us the message of reconciliation. [20]We are therefore Christ's ambassadors, as though God were making his appeal through us. We implore you on Christ's behalf: Be reconciled to God.

Nurture the gifts in others

As mature Christians we should be sensitive to the giftings that are in new believers the same way a parent would discern the strengths and talents of his or her children. No two people have them exactly the same. Each person has got unique qualities and spiritual giftings given by God. As my fingerprints are different from anyone else's, so are my giftings. Even though I may have the same gift as you, we may manifest it differently because we are different. I am emphasizing individuality. Each of us is created so intricately special with gifts and talents and personality etc. The gift of prophecy in me is not the same as the gift of prophecy in someone else. There are some things the same, but the expression is as unique as each snowflake or fingerprint.

The amazing thing is that we are earthen vessels, our bodies are flesh and blood and God's Spirit lives in us. Once we leave the body, it dies. Your spirit is the essence of you. Once your spirit – that has a human soul – leaves the physical body – it dies. Our essence is the life of the body. The Holy Spirit living in us uses us even though we are imperfect. A new Christian will discover more about himself or herself because of God's presence living in him or her. A new Christian will begin to develop spiritual discernment. It is the most important thing because discerning God's voice is necessary for all future development.

As a new Christian, the Holy Spirit prompted me to get rid of all occult and other Eastern religious books I had collect. I knew I had to burn them. No one told me. The Spirit of God prompted me. There were hundreds of dollars worth of books, but I knew I did not want those things anymore. I chose Christ. I told this to those who lead me to the Lord what I had done, and they showed me the Scripture Acts 19: 19 and explained to me that it was necessary to rid myself of all other gods or things that are used by other gods. I began to pray for myself "God let me love what you love and hate what you hate." As I yielded myself to the Holy Spirit, He instructed me, gave me wisdom, discernment etc. I knew that the Scriptures were true but my life up until my salvation had been lived as a non-Christian, so I had to learn the scriptures, so I knew God's way of doing things. The Bible is our manual for life. The Scripture teaches us all that we must know to apply to all areas of our lives. It is not simply reading it with head knowledge but getting the word engrafted into our souls that brings true transformation. (James 1: 21)

He doesn't call you as a servant only, but He calls you as a son (Galatians 4:7). God calls you as his own child. He lives in you and He instructs you with all love so as a parent trains his or her child. In Corinthians 12, he calls you a part of the Body of Christ. The more you learn about God, the more you want to learn about Him. You start a relationship, the day you become a Christian. You begin falling in love with God. The more you know Him, the more you love Him. His love surpasses all earthly measurement.

Ephesians 3: [18] may have power, together with all the Lord's holy people, to grasp how wide and long and high and deep is the love of Christ, [19] and to know this love that surpasses knowledge—that you may be filled to the measure of all the fullness of God.

Relationship with Christ

Relationship with God is falling in love. If you have never experienced falling in love, you will not understand this compassion. Falling in love with God is learning more about Him. The more you receive His mercy, the more you receive His forgiveness, His love, the more you love Him. His agape love towards us begins to win our hearts so that our hearts are filled with his love.

You can only truly love God with God's love. Human love can be tremendous but there is a limit. There are people who will say "That's the last straw. I'm cutting you out of my life." There is an end of human love. But the agape love of God is unconditional. God forgives and always will as long as we return to Him. If you sin, run towards God not away from Him (Kenneth Copeland taught this, and it changed my life). Running to God first, is always the answer. Jesus blood was shed once and for all. Jesus Christ already paid the price for any sins: past, present or future. When Jesus uttered the words "It is finished" It was the final solution. Jesus blood cleanses from all sin. His unconditional love towards us overwhelms us because we can't believe He is that good, but He is.

God does not have love – He is love. He is the essence of it. He doesn't have mercy – He is mercy. God is the essence of all virtue and grace. We don't deserve it – we cannot earn it – we can receive it by Christ as a gift – it is free – but we must go to God in prayer. That is the only aspect necessary to receiving forgiveness.

It is like the love a parent feels towards his or her child. It is similar to the passion of falling in love because you think of the person and want to be with him or her. You start falling in love with God, you will want more and more of His presence, His Word, His body. You will identify with Him. Relationship with God is more intimate than any other relationship because God lives inside of you. It is not an obsession. It is a passion. It is learning to love him with His love. It is learning to care about the things He cares about. It is learning to hate the things He hates.

As a new Christian my first compelling drive was to share the truth of what happened to me with all the people I knew were not going to heaven. That was everybody I knew because I wasn't headed towards God, I was going in the opposite direction. I began telling them how awesome God is and sharing how He transformed my life. Some got saved immediately. Many wanted nothing to do with me. Some thought it would pass away just as my pursuit of God through many other religions were all temporary. My desire to share with them was not human love alone. It was the love of God, the mercy of God towards them wanting them to be saved. I knew they were seeking joy, pleasure, wisdom, relief, fascination etc. but they were looking in the wrong areas. I wanted them to know Jesus is the way – the only way, the truth and the life (John 14: 16). I knew the peace of God that replaced my old self. I knew the joy that bubbled up from the fountain of Christ living in me – I wanted them to know God, so they could know eternal life. The goodness of God cannot be explained with words, but I knew they knew my old self and they could see the difference. I believed it would be enough to cause them all to become Christians.

It was tough for me to understand how they could reject Christ. It was tough to lose many of the people who had been close to me, but I knew I no longer wanted to go any other way – I chose Christ. I chose a different life. I chose the Word of God. My life was radically changed. At first the only Christians I knew were the ones who lead me to the LORD and the ones I brought to Christ.

Being a Christian is not a religious thing. It is a relationship. On forms that ask for religion I'd like to put none, but they wouldn't understand so I put Christian. I do not advocate religion. I studied many world religions and the occult before I became a Christian. Jesus Christ living in me is the main difference. Encountering a true and living God is what causes me to keep on serving, giving, living for Christ. It's not a one-time occurrence – Christ is always with me – living inside of me. It transforms a life. I began to view the world differently. Suddenly I had tremendous love towards Christians. I had mocked Christians before I became a Christian. I didn't know it was true. I didn't know but as soon as I became a Christian and was in a church, I started feeling love towards all the people around me who believed the same. As I met more Christians, I began to realize that Christians could be plumbers, truck drivers, professors, high ranking officials, teachers, executives etc. I was surprised because I had believed the lie that Christians were ignorant. It is the message the secular media usually presents; a false view of Christianity.

The Agape Love

Experiencing the agape love of God – is overwhelming. Christians will be fascinated with the multisided beauty of God for all eternity. As a crystal or diamond shows light in many facets, so is God's beauty. As you turn the crystal or diamond, light shines differently on the different aspects of it in a beautiful way. As soon as you start to think you know something about God, there is new revelation of Him. He is dynamic, Charismatic, passionate. The more you learn about Him the more you want to learn about Him. That is why I use the comparison of falling in love. It is developing the most intimate exciting relationship a person can develop.

God's Word revealed to us by The Holy Spirit shows us God. Each scripture brings a new truth of His nature or His beauty. The more of the Word of

God we get into us, the more we are transformed. God wants His Word to be so much in us that it is engrafted into our very soul (James 1:21). We get the Word of God on the inside of us so that we become as living epistles. It is not simply memorizing Scripture. We become the scripture. We live it with our lives. We personify it.

Chapter 1 Questions

1. What are the earliest memories you have of Christians in the Church? Describe them.
2. Write your testimony of becoming a Christian. Read it over and add in all people who influenced you to become a Christian even if they were not the ones to directly pray with you.
3. Describe your relationship with those who mentored you in Christ. What did they do purposefully to encourage you as a Christian?
4. Pray that you might disciple someone in the Church. Believe God will prompt you and ask the person to join you in some type of Christian ministry experience.

2 THE WORD OF GOD

The Word of God living in us – shines the light of the gospel to those around us. They realize something is different about us, but they don't understand. They may ask us why we respond that way or why we do something. We are living by the Word of God, we are living by the Scriptures. We are living how God wants all people to live by the scriptures.

Although there are some common truths to a Christian and a non- Christian that is the only similarity – physical and natural communality. The main difference is in the origin of self. As Christians, we are no longer living under the sun. We are no longer subject to the sin of Adam. We live in the realm of the supernatural. We are reigning with the Son of God who is seated on the Throne in Glory. The same Spirit that dwells in Christ, dwells in us. As we learn the scripture we become the scripture. We apply it to all areas of our lives. We become a living Word – an example to those around us. We might be the only Christians someone meets. It might cause someone to want to know more of God.

Matthew 13: ³Then he told them many things in parables, saying: "A farmer went out to sow his seed. ⁴As he was scattering the seed, some fell along the path, and the birds came and ate it up. ⁵Some fell on rocky places, where it did not have much soil. It sprang up quickly, because the soil was shallow. ⁶But when the sun came up, the plants were scorched, and they withered because they had no root. ⁷Other seed fell among thorns, which grew up and choked the plants. ⁸Still other seed fell on good soil, where it produced a crop—a hundred, sixty or thirty times what was sown. ⁹Whoever has ears, let them hear."

Sowing Seed is sowing the Word of God (Luke 8:11). The ground cannot be hard like stoney ground, or the roots cannot grow. The plant will die. The ground cannot be on a path or they cannot get rooted. The seed cannot be among thorns because the weeds will choke the life out of the good plant. The soil must be soft, crumbly, no stones, not clay, not too sandy – it must be workable. Rich soil is fertilized. The seed that gets in that type of soil will root, grow and flourish. Nutrients are in the soil giving the plant all necessary life to grow and mature. The Seed is the same. The earth determines the growth of the seed.

The Hundred-Fold

Jesus explains to His disciples that the Word of God is the seed. Our hearts must be soft, as rich crumbly earth ready to receive the seed. If we are hard hearted, God's Word will not produce fruit. God will not violate human will. If there are stones or obstacles or anything that separates us from God in our hearts, we cannot profit from God's Word fully. If there are cares and other things in our heart, as weeds they prevent God's Word from growing. Our hearts must be as good soil. We should be soft, ready to receive God's Word, believe it and receive it as though it were the most valuable, precious thing given to us, the word will take root and grow and flourish. Our hearts must be ready to receive God's Word. Ground doesn't determine its own quality. People can change the soil of their hearts. I myself started gardening in clay soil so thick, I used some of it to create pottery. To prepare it for planting, I took out the stones and the weeds. I added fertilizer and compost and sand and over the years my soil became a rich crumbly black soil.

Human will determines the soil condition of the human heart. A person can choose God's Word as most important. We prepare our hearts by prayer, praise, worship, reading God's Word. We must continuously, be doing this to keep our hearts ready to receive from God's Word. Only a human wholly seeking God's Word as treasure can receive fruit from it. It could mean praying saying "Yes – I receive this word and God let it produce in me 100 fold, 1000 fold increase after its kind." Because God wants us to produce fruit. The Word of God can be applied to all aspects of our human lives. The Word of God such as the following can apply to all areas of your life.

Psalm 37: 4Take delight in the LORD,
   and he will give you the desires of your heart.

If you plant one pea seed, a pea plant can grow up to produce many pea pods. A kernel of corn planted can produce 3 or 4 heads of corn on it. A seed is multiplied by your planting it. It always produces after it's kind. A pea seed will always produce peas. A corn kernel always produces corn. It's the way God designed all vegetation and animal life to reproduce. In the same way, God wants to multiply the Word of God in your life.

This can apply to my finances. I put God first in my giving and He can bless me financially beyond what I know or have known. This can apply to my life in terms of Spiritual growth. I desire to know Jesus in His resurrection glory. As I pursue Him, He can reveal Himself to me in His glory, more and more. The word can apply to my life as I am grocery shopping. There is something I want, God can enable me to receive it or obtain it. It can apply to me in my career. I can pray for the job I desire, and get the education and training and God can give be supernatural favour and opportunity to obtain the job.

God's Word can apply to all areas of my life. That is a 100-fold blessing on the Word of God. It can be yours also. Receive the Word of God with gladness and rejoicing. Receive it and pray that God will let it apply to all areas of your life. We determine the quality of the soil in our hearts. God will never force you to receive from Him. God's will for us is to prosper us in all aspects of our lives (Deuteronomy 28) but we must believe it and receive it.

All things are possible to those who believe that God is and is a rewarder of those who diligently seek Him (Hebrews 11: 6)

God's word can impact all areas of our lives. Even though you may not be able to openly witness in your workplace, you can serve in your career with excellence. You can be kind, compassionate, diligent, prudent etc. People can see the fruit of The Holy Spirit in us as we serve Christ through our excellence and want to know God because of it. Christians can serve God in all aspects of human life. God's Word produces in us godly character, the fruit of the Spirit, Christlikeness.

Gal 5: [22] But the fruit of the Spirit is love, joy, peace, forbearance, kindness, goodness, faithfulness, [23] gentleness and self-control. Against such things there is no law.

Colossians 3: [23] Whatever you do, work at it with all your heart, as working for the Lord, not for human masters, [24] since you know that you will receive an inheritance from the Lord as a reward. It is the Lord Christ you are serving.

God's Word in you always

A person can be exercising or running in a race, Christ is there with you. He strengthens you, helps you and as you do your best in all areas of life, you are honouring God. Please receive the truth that being a Christian is 24/7- 365. Christ in us, His empowering presence – not only in Church or home but in all areas of life. God wants us to enjoy our lives. As we live with Him in us, honour Him by doing our best, giving our best effort and giving Him all the glory – we honour God. The fruits of righteousness will be evident to those around us. Christians should be so excellent that people come to us to want to know why we are succeeding, why we are joyful, why we are excellent etc. Our prioritizing God's Word, honouring God will cause us to be attractors of people.

The Holy Spirit living in me is the best life I could ever get. The Holy Spirit leads, guides, encourages, brings scriptures to my remembrance, cheers me on. People pay much money for personal trainers and life coaches. I know they can make a difference to people but The Holy Spirit in me coaching me, training me for reigning in the Kingdom of God is the best life coach I've experienced. The Holy Spirit empowers me to do everyday things such as washing laundry or mowing the lawn. In all areas of life, I can excel because of Christ living in me.

When I pray for wisdom from God, I pray for a 100-fold blessing on it.

James 3: [17] But the wisdom that comes from heaven is first of all pure; then peace-loving, considerate, submissive, full of mercy and good fruit, impartial and sincere.

I want wisdom in making big decisions, Yes, but I also want wisdom in daily life while I'm doing business, or driving my car or in giving excellent service to the people I'm providing the service for. I want God to use me in all areas of my life. I want me heart to always be ready to receive from God or to give or help someone.

A person sold out to God is always ready for service; Semper paratis (always ready). It means keeping your heart right with God always. If you sin, repent immediately – receive the cleansing from sin from Jesus and go on with your life in freedom. In the unique qualities God has placed within you, you a member of the body of Christ, God will show Himself in the earth. God will use your character, your qualities, your education, your training, everything about you to reveal His glory through your life.

Chapter 2 Questions
1. Describe the importance of Bible reading in your life and any changes that have occurred.
2. God can speak to us in different ways. What are the primary ways God speaks to you?
3. Once God has spoken to you, what is your response? Do you always share it? Do you never share it? Describe what you do.

3 GOD CAN USE YOU

Not everyone is outgoing. There are timid people. God can use them through their kind deeds and their giving or serving. God can use all types of people. I've known of people who are shut ins, they are not well enough to go to church, but they write encouraging cards and letters to people, encouraging the Body of Christ. There are people who pass out gospel tracts to every person who comes to their home or in the grocery stores. They are agents of righteousness. God can use you whether you are strong, an extravert or strong but timid. God can use you in your weakness. I know of a senior who was in hospital who preached to every person who came in her room.

God can use you. Let your heart be ready to receive. Let your heart be ready to serve. It is a matter of choice. Each day we can set our course much like on a ship or on a plane, they chart their journey. We can do it with prayer and praise and with obedience to the Holy Spirit's promptings and leadings throughout the day.

Psalm 113: ³ From the rising of the sun to the place where it sets,
   the name of the LORD is to be praised.

Let that psalm be your prayer. Present yourself to God each day so that God can shine the glory of God through you in your ordinary life. God can use you to reach people no one else can reach. Your sphere of authority is all the people in your life and your unique relationship with them You increase your reach by giving and praying for others.

Members of The Church

Your individuality

The Holy Spirit shines through us in our uniqueness. We should ask God to use us in the gifts we know of. If you enjoy serving, pray that God will give you opportunities to serve. Should you be in a local church, opportunities abound for you to use this gift. Use the gifts you know you have and pray for opportunities. As you discover new gifts, pray for opportunities to use them. Expect God to use you in your career. Should you be a plumber, do it with excellence and expect there may be opportunities for you to pray with people, encourage people or give a discount to someone for your service. All of these are ways God can use ordinary jobs to manifest His glory. It flows through you. You are the carrier of God's glory.

I got saved as a student in my early 20's. Accepting Christ was explained to me as a most serious thing. It was total abandonment – total surrender. I was willing to give all of myself to God. I would have done anything to become a Christian as soon as I realized Jesus was my Saviour. After I prayed to accept Christ, I asked those who prayed with me if I could keep going to school because I was a student. They assured me, I could. I didn't know anything about being a Christian. I didn't know God would use me right where I was and that I didn't have to obtain something on my own. I received Him as Saviour and LORD and He used me in my studies. I spoke with other students. I invited people to my home. I met other Christians. Mostly I was a witness by being excellent, kind, diligent, respectful etc.

1 Corinthians 7: [20] Each person should remain in the situation they were in when God called them.

God usually wants to use you right in the place you are at. There are instances when you might feel a prompting to go preach as an evangelist travelling or a missionary etc. But true of myself was God wanted me to get as much education as possible. The more education I obtained opened new opportunities for me. I could do more because the degrees were as keys to new opportunities. The more training and skill one gets, including things such as certificates and diplomas and drivers licences, gets him or her more opportunities to do earthly things. The more things we can do, the more we can shine the glory of God into all areas of society.

There are Christian athletes, Christian scholars, Christian clerks, Christian singers, Christian politicians, Christian technologists. God can use you in all the spheres of society you are in. This involves your hobbies and interests as well as your career. You could coach baseball or hockey and share Christ through your serving children. (Please read my book on Spheres of Authority for more details on this.)

Spiritual Gifts

Children and teens and youth should pursue God for their giftings and callings. Their Christian parents or someone with more experience as a Christian should pray for them and also speak to them about the gifts and talents they recognize in them. Youth should see where their aptitudes are as well as their interests. Christian parents should be praying over their children concerning this also. God can direct you into the place you best fit. It will be something you love. It is what your strengths are and what you enjoy the most. God takes pleasure in giving you the things you most love. Just as a Parent delights in giving good things to his or her children, God delights in our joy and our success.

Spiritual Mentors

Often pastors or leaders in the church will recognize the giftings in the children and youth of the congregation and help them develop those gifts. As a new Christian, there was a Christian couple who discipled me in a Bible class for the foundations of our faith. Afterwards, they adopted me as part of their family. They recognized my passion for God. They encouraged me as a Christian and spoke with me, bought me a concordance and taught me to use it. They invited me to their home. After the first year of their discipling me, they got me to take offerings in class and organize things. They got me to pray for the people, got me involved in outreach ministries. They kept training me as a disciple, but they also witnessed to me how Christian families do things. They always held hands and prayed over the meal as a family. They always spoke about Jesus no matter what the occasion was. They invested themselves in me. They honoured me by calling me daughter. They were as my spiritual family. They trained me to teach and preach. Once they started a new church, they got me to preach. They kept on pouring into me. This was essential to me as a Christian. They purposely and prayerfully invested in my life. They got me to use my spiritual gifts and talents. They encouraged me by their overwhelming love towards me.

God will provide mentors to those who do not have Christian parents. It' something new Christians should pray for. As we lead someone to Christ, it is something we should pray for or prepare to do. New Christians are the most willing people to use in the

Church. They are easily trained and willing to serve. We should recruit them as ushers or greeters or helpers in other ministries. The more active they are in church life, the more they will learn about Christ. I was a willing servant. As I served in one area, such as helping wash dishes, clearing tables, practical things, God let me meet the most excellent people who I might never have met had I not volunteered. I made friends of all ages because of it. I served in practical areas such as kitchen duties, later I prayed with people, encouraged people with scriptures, became a Sunday school teacher, preached in churches – all because people invested in me. They discipled me. I continued serving as part of my life. I felt the church was my church and I cared about all aspects of it. In one church, I planted a flower garden. It was something I desired to do. I got the pastor's permission and did it.

Making Disciples

New Christians should be encouraged to start serving in the church. They can learn from the more mature Christians around them. They can make friends. They can also contribute as well as serve. They shouldn't be the pastors or teachers of the church, but they can be trained to be servants and taught Christian work ethic and also enjoy people of all ages by volunteering or being recruited. Don't dump all the work on the new Christians, but involve them.

You bond with people you pray with, worship with, wash dishes with, mow the lawn with and do practical things with. They become closer than blood relatives (that are not saved) because of your shared lives. You form friendships with people you teach Sunday school with. You become knit into the local church body and experience a deep sense of belonging.

Bible study

Christian Adult Bible classes are also necessary in the local church. There are some, but it should be a priority – bible study. It can be on the Sunday or on a different day. As there are mature elders and deacons and teachers in a church, it doesn't mean the pastor must do all the teaching and preaching. Mega churches, large churches of more than 1000 members, can offer more variety than smaller churches. The more people, the more diversity of Bible class choices should be given. I myself experienced a variety of classes from foundations, Spiritual gifts teacher's training, eventually ministers. Candidate school. There were classes in Hebrew and Greek as well as praise and worship. There were classes for all ages. Our churches should be training centres for excellence in all aspects of Bible studies.

Since I became a Christian, my church has always been the centre of my social life as well as my spiritual life. It is easy to make friends with people who you play baseball with or go to class picnics with. It is easy to make friends with people you serve breakfast to or wash dishes with. Many people come to Christ need immersion in the Body of Christ. Our Churches must be places of praise, worship, preaching, teaching, serving, giving as well as discipleship. Our church should be our family. We should feel connected to them and with them. One of my churches invested and purchased an athletic centre so family events and activities could be held there. It is also such an excellent facility that when open to the public, people come and it can be a place of witnessing to those who come.

People who come to Christ with a non-Christian background can sit at banquets or breakfasts and talk with other Christians. They will begin to develop a sense of the difference between Christian life and life without Christ. The discipling is not for youth alone. Anyone who comes to Christ must experience Christian life so he or she can raise his or her family in a godly Christian way.

I met a man who was in his late 80's who had become a Christian. He drove for almost 2 hours to get to our church and always came. I am so glad for the chance I got to speak with him. He impressed me tremendously by his devotion to God and his willingness to travel that distance to get to a church where he could learn about Christ.

Chapter 3 Questions
1. What is your role in your church? Write it.
2. What is your goal in ministry? Write it.
3. Describe what you believe to be your main callings. Include your spiritual gifts and how they can assist you in serving Christ.

4 CHURCH GATHERINGS

There should be fellowship activities in the church also for all ages such as picnics, dinners, events, activities. Children can learn more by hanging out with other Christian children than they can by only going to Sunday school. I myself was pretty involved in raising my niece and my nephew because both their parents worked, and I was often home first because I am a teacher. I would do activities with them, but I also got together with Christian families with children of the same age so that they could know what Christian children are like. I felt a strong desire to get them some Christian friends. People only learn what it is like to be a Christian by hanging around with Christians. It should motivate us to be good examples to those around us. It should motivate us to involve new Christians in family and fun activities as well as Bible study and discipleship.

The most essential thing for a new Christian is to get into the Word of God in Bible study and preaching and teaching from a local church and they discover their Spiritual gifts and begin to use them. Pray for people to disciple others. Pray that God would use more mature Christians to "adopt" a new Christian as part of their family. The more the new Christian is involved in serving and Christian life, the more he or she will develop Christian values and life choices.

2 Timothy 2: [15] Do your best to present yourself to God as one approved, a worker who does not need to be ashamed and who correctly handles the word of truth

In one of my churches I literally helped to build the church, laying cement and bricks, putting up drywall, and doping other practical things. I worked along side the pastors everyday until it was complete. It was months. I developed friendship with them and work ethic beyond what I've ever known. They would work all day doing cement or other construction tasks and then clean up and preach at the night service. I felt so knit in that local body of Christ that I never would have left it. I knew most of the congregation.

The pastors invested in me, involving me in teaching and preaching as well as other areas of responsibility such as running the church bookstore. It was my pleasure to serve in the church; it really was my spiritual family. They were so welcoming that they accepted me and promoted me. I believed fully that I could pray, seek God and share it with the pastors and they would pray about it and approve it accordingly. I trusted the leadership because they were led by the Holy Spirit.

One of the pastors had been radically saved and delivered from drugs and alcohol. He had a special heart for men who were in addictions. He would often preach and pray with people on the street bringing all the youth group to witness to people. One of the young men who got saved came to our church with drug addiction. My pastor would get him early in the morning and get him to work along side of us during the day while we were building the church. He would serve him dinner, invited him to his home and would drop him off at night. He discipled many men in that way by one on one discipleship, relationship with them until they were set free from addictions and living free as Christians. By investing in others in this way, sharing your very life with them, people can experience Christian life as compared to the life of someone living on the street.

A Serving Church

The level of volunteers or willing servants in a church is a pretty good gage of the maturity of the church. I've been part of some churches where we would cook and serve the food for a member's funeral. We would do it all because the member was part of us. The pastor would ask for servants and right away people would either raise their hand or stand to donate their efforts. It could mean cooking, cleaning, serving. There were always more than enough volunteers. That is the sign of a growing church, a thriving church. All the parts of the body are coming into agreement with the need presented.

Psalm 100 : 2 Worship the LORD with gladness;
  come before him with joyful songs.

1 Corinthians 10: 31 So whether you eat or drink or whatever you do, do it all for the glory of God. 32 Do not cause anyone to stumble, whether Jews, Greeks or the church of God— 33 even as I try to please everyone in every way. For I am not seeking my own good but the good of many, so that they may be saved.

Colossians 3: 17 And whatever you do, whether in word or deed, do it all in the name of the Lord Jesus, giving thanks to God the Father through him.

Chapter 4 Study Questions
1. Does your current church host special gatherings? List them and describe them. List any others you have experienced in the churches you've been in.
2. How important were those gatherings to you? Did you volunteer? Were you involved in ministry?
3. Should you become a Christian minister, what special gatherings would you propose as special gatherings. Describe your role, the people who would assist you and the ultimate goal of the gatherings.

5 SERVING

The Church must build up itself by the serving and giving and gifts of the Holy Spirit within the church and linking with other churches. The church must also exist for evangelism and discipleship as well as missions.

Because the church should be an organism – a living body rather than an organization, the parts of the Body of Christ should come together should there be a need in the church. I experienced this quality in all the churches I've been in but there was a particular small (200 member) church I was a part of that was particularly a serving church. Someone who was moving requested help. There were so many people who volunteered to help them move, we moved the family within several hours. People volunteered to make refreshments for all who participated in the move and the family didn't need to cook that day. Someone else bought a home and requested help with painting. Once more there were so many people volunteering as a cell group that it was painted within a day. There were elders and deacons that would minister to anyone assisting the pastors with prayer meetings, speaking, serving communion, visitation. The body of the church was strong. The members were knit together for the benefit of the body and the building up of the church.

Ephesians 4: [11] So Christ himself gave the apostles, the prophets, the evangelists, the pastors and teachers, [12] to equip his people for works of service, so that the body of Christ may be built up [13] until we all reach unity in the faith and in the knowledge of the Son of God and become mature, attaining to the whole measure of the fullness of Christ.

The pastors view of the church body was imparted vision to the elders and deacons who also imparted it into the church members. You served because you should; a member of the body had a need so we all responded with service.

I would describe the body as a comparison to the human body. I am a carpenter's daughter, and have done some bits of carpentry, but I don't boast in them. On occasion I would hit my thumb. My first response was to suck it to relieve the pain. My eyes examined it – to discern the seriousness of it. All of my body was affected by the one member's need. The Thumb – not always valued for its importance was getting all my body to relieve it from its need. One member of the body of Christ matters in the same importance within a church body. This is not only important in small churches but can be in large churches as long as the church is connected with cell groups, classes etc. so there is a network of relationships spanning all members of the church.

Prayer

That same serving church, would come together as regular churches twice a week but when the pastor was deathly ill, all the church responded by gathering together each night to pray for his healing. There was a deep love and respect for the shepherd of the church. People brought their children. Hundreds of people sacrificed to gather to intercede for the pastor. It was serving but in a prayer way. It was a particular need that required serious intervention should our pastor live because it wasn't expected that he would. It was the same body gathering to meet a need. Our pastor lived defeating all odds and doctor's proclamations. It was a miracle we received from God.

The only way a church can get an identity as a serving church in this way is should the pastors have strong vision of the church and her role, and there be elders and deacons in positions of authority. It must be imparted to the people so that each person felt a part of the body. No one ignored another's needs. Each church family rallied around other church families as a support system. Whether the need was spiritual or practical – the body of Christ responded with deep devotion without seeking any reward except the benefit of the family they were serving. It is similar to the way that the Prophet Nehemiah rallied the Israelites to rebuild the walls of Jerusalem with the gates etc. They worked, each family assigned to their particular section, building, ready to fight off any who opposed them, devoted to the corporate vision – the rebuilding of the walls of Jerusalem.

Nehemiah 4: [16] From that day on, half of my men did the work, while the other half were equipped with spears, shields, bows and armor. The officers posted themselves behind all the people of Judah [17] who were building the wall. Those who carried materials did their work with one hand and held a weapon in the other, [18] and each of the builders wore his sword at his side as he worked. But the man who sounded the trumpet stayed with me.

Chapter 5 study questions

1. Describe your impression of Jesus Christ as servant. Include at least 1 scripture. Describe how it proves he was a servant.
2. In what areas of the Church have you served? What areas did you continue in and why?
3. In your role in the Church, how important is your serving? Is it a strong motivation for you?
4. How could you serve most effectively in a local Church or within the Church globally?

6 THE LOCAL CHURCH:
THE UNIVERSAL CHURCH

It is important to be a part of the local church functioning together as a strong body. There must also be care for the universal church or the global church. This can be accomplished through giving towards missions, sending missionaries, training up ministers and launching them into ministry, praying for the nations and assisting other churches in our region.

Missions

All of the churches I've been a part of were strong in missionary giving. There was not only the view of helping each other but in preaching Christ to the nations. Often missionaries would be church members who sacrificed their vacations to serve in some missionary endeavor such as evangelising through drams and concerts and crusades (preaching and worship as well as literally building church buildings for people in other nations. Missionaries raised their own support; the church would also take up a collection for them. Different departments of the church youth, children, etc. would raise finances to donate through car washes, bake sales, concerts etc. All the church would support the missionaries knowing that it was Christ's commission we were partnering with.

Mark 16: *15 He said to them, "Go into all the world and preach the gospel to all creation. 16 Whoever believes and is baptized will be saved, but whoever does not believe will be condemned. 17 And these signs will accompany those who believe: In my name they will drive out demons; they will speak in new tongues; 18 they will pick up snakes with their hands; and when they drink deadly poison, it will not hurt them at all; they will place their hands on sick people, and they will get well."*

Partnering with other churches in different countries

In our multicultural church, we had many people from Central and South America. They all had family members in those nations so should any tragedy arise in those nations, we immediately responded. We would take up collections of items to be donated to the sister church in a different nation. It was not a wealthy church but people, families, brought clothing, canned goods, things that could be shipped to help the Church in the other nation. What was excellent about it is that it was efficient, precise and quick. The stuff was gathered, packed shipped – all by volunteers.

1 Corinthians 16: 1 Now about the collection for the Lord's people: Do what I told the Galatian churches to do. 2 On the first day of every week, each one of you should set aside a sum of money in keeping with

your income, saving it up, so that when I come no collections will have to be made.

Missions

In large churches, we should also encourage it also. There were always collections taken for missionaries. Often, they were invited to speak in our churches, give a presentation of what they were doing in the other nations. It included feeding programs as well as Biblical studies. Some missionaries would go to pastor or assist pastors in other nations. There were always groups who went as a team to evangelize with dramas, music, Bible classes.

Some sacrificed large North American salaries to go do similar jobs in other nations so they could preach Christ there. As they would speak about the practical needs they were meeting as well as the spiritual, I would hang on the edge of my chair wishing I could be there. Some were digging wells of water for people in nations that were very poor. Some were teaching hygiene as well as Bible classes. The more personal the connection to the missionary, the stronger the support for the missionary. People who know a member of their church has sacrificed to go serve in other nations, will be quicker to give because they know the life of the missionary and the integrity of him or her.

1 Thessalonians 5: [12] Now we ask you, brothers and sisters, to acknowledge those who work hard among you, who care for you in the Lord and who admonish you. [13] Hold them in the highest regard in love because of their work. Live in peace with each other.

Collections for missions were not only finances. Various groups within the church contributed. There were seniors who would crochet things. There were women who sewed. There were men who were skilled in the trades who volunteered to help design, build and oversea the construction of new buildings in other nations. Once more it was a response of the whole local church body coming together to serve a community so that the Church global could be built up.

Community Evangelism

Not all people have a strong overt personality. Some are more timid or quiet, but all can take part in evangelism. Hosting concerts at a church building is a way of bringing in people who might never come to church any other way. There was always attendance way beyond what was expected. There was always an altar call. Many Christian musicians and bands openly talk about church. Some of them preach as well as invite people to pray with them.

We would pass out free tickets to the concert or event (also dramas) and go door to door inviting people within the community. There would be some type of refreshment served. It was a way of getting people in the door. We would pray over the event and do it as an offering to God knowing that only God could save a soul. Winning people to Christ was our main objective. Those more timid, could pass out programs or serve coffee. Those more outgoing could be the Master of ceremonies for the event. All of us would go in pairs, recruiting the community.

I especially enjoyed evangelizing door to door by singing Christmas carols. We would sing. People would answer their doors and try to give us money. We wouldn't take any money but instead we would give them some small gift such as a pen or a nick knack. We always gave them something with the church's contact information on it. We offered to pray for them for any need. There were not many who did not take the pen or item we offered them. Some asked us to pray with them about family situations. More than once, I was greeted by someone in tears who was glad to have someone pray with him or her about a particular thing.

1 Timothy 4: [2] Preach the word; be prepared in season and out of season; correct, rebuke and encourage—with great patience and careful instruction

The church inviting the community to dramas and musicals etc. develops a reputation for the church. The church becomes more than a sign over a building, but people who might not come to church would consider coming because we met them, prayed with them and invited them. They realize we are no different than ordinary people, but we genuinely care for them.

A Thriving Church

A strong healthy church is members connected to each other. The gifts of the spirit are in the church. The fruit of the Spirit is in the Church evidenced by all the members coming together to build up the church body. There is care for churches and Christians in other nations and there is evangelism in their community. There is connectedness with other churches in the community sponsoring large events. There is communication with other churches by the pastors joining together to pray for their churches corporately as well as for the community to come to Christ.

All of the spheres must come together apostles, prophets, evangelists, pastors teachers.

Chapter 6 Study Questions

1. List your main manifestational, motivational and ministry gifts. If you do not know them, do a survey or get a book on the topic (My book on Spiritual gifts is available on amazon in either paperback or kindle edition). It is necessary for you to know the giftings God has given you.
2. Write the Prophetic words or prayers over your life.
3. In your studies of ministry (or in your studies towards ministries) describe the most important topics you have experience with, and you believe must be imparted to others.

7 THE JERUSALEM CHURCH

The last appearance of Jesus in his resurrected body on earth was at the Mt. of Olives where he appeared with over 500 witnesses there. He instructed them briefly that the gift of the Holy Spirit would come. They went to Jerusalem to wait for it. This is in direct fulfillment of his words to his disciples.

John 14: 25 "All this I have spoken while still with you. 26 But the Advocate, the Holy Spirit, whom the Father will send in my name, will teach you all things and will remind you of everything I have said to you. 27 Peace I leave with you; my peace I give you. I do not give to you as the world gives. Do not let your hearts be troubled and do not be afraid.

Jesus was ascending into heaven surrounded by angels. His last words to the disciples was to obey him by waiting – praying at Jerusalem until they received the gift of the Holy Spirit.

Acts 1:4 On one occasion, while he was eating with them, he gave them this command: "Do not leave Jerusalem, but wait for the gift my Father promised, which you have heard me speak about. 5 For John baptized with[a] water, but in a few days you will be baptized with[b] the Holy Spirit."

⁶Then they gathered around him and asked him, "Lord, are you at this time going to restore the kingdom to Israel?"

⁷He said to them: "It is not for you to know the times or dates the Father has set by his own authority. ⁸But you will receive power when the Holy Spirit comes on you; and you will be my witnesses in Jerusalem, and in all Judea and Samaria, and to the ends of the earth."

Of all who heard him and saw him visibly ascend into heaven surrounded by angels, 120 obeyed him and went to pray until the Holy Spirit came. They did not know what it was. It was new. They had not experienced it before. They obeyed anyway.

BAPTISM OF THE HOLY SPIRIT

The apostles who stayed and prayed not knowing what would occur. The Birth of the church at Jerusalem was direct obedience to Jesus. It did not come immediately. As they prayed and expected to receive from God, suddenly the gift of the Holy Spirit was given.

Acts 2: 1 When the day of Pentecost came, they were all together in one place.²Suddenly a sound like the blowing of a violent wind came from heaven and filled the whole house where they were sitting. ³They saw what seemed to be tongues of fire that separated and came to rest on each of them. [4]All of them were filled with the Holy Spirit and began to speak in other tongues[a] as the Spirit enabled them.

The disciples received the gift of the Holy Spirit and began speaking in other tongues worshipping and praising God. The Holy Spirit had filled their spirits so that they were worshipping God and praising God with might in languages they had never been taught. They were speaking by the direct unction of the Holy Spirit. The anointing or presence of God in them and upon them was so strong that it compelled them to go into the streets praising God and prophesying in languages they had never studied. There were many pilgrims gathered at Jerusalem for the feast. They came from all nations to worship at Jerusalem. There were crowds of them in the street.

Acts 2: [5]Now there were staying in Jerusalem God-fearing Jews from every nation under heaven. [6]When they heard this sound, a crowd came together in bewilderment, because each one heard their own language being spoken. [7]Utterly amazed, they asked: "Aren't all these who are speaking Galileans? [8]Then how is it that each of us hears them in our native language? [9]Parthians, Medes and Elamites; residents of Mesopotamia, Judea and Cappadocia, Pontus and Asia,[b] [10]Phrygia and Pamphylia, Egypt and the parts of Libya near Cyrene; visitors from Rome[11] (both Jews and converts to Judaism); Cretans and Arabs—we hear them declaring the wonders of God in our own tongues!" ¹²Amazed and perplexed, they asked one another, "What does this mean?"

Some of the pilgrims wondered how these uneducated fishermen could be praising God in their own languages knowing they couldn't have learned the languages of the nations. They were interested to know the reason for this strange phenomenon. Some people blamed it on them being drunk. Peter was inspired to preach top the crowd the first Holy Spirit sermon ever preached. He explained that it was the gift of the Holy Spirit as promised in Joel 2:28.

Acts 2: ¹⁴Then Peter stood up with the Eleven, raised his voice and addressed the crowd: "Fellow Jews and all of you who live in Jerusalem, let me explain this to you; listen carefully to what I say. ¹⁵These people are not drunk, as you suppose. It's only nine in the morning! ¹⁶No, this is what was spoken by the prophet Joel:

¹⁷"'In the last days, God says,
    I will pour out my Spirit on all people.
Your sons and daughters will prophesy,
    your young men will see visions,
    your old men will dream dreams.
¹⁸Even on my servants, both men and women,
    I will pour out my Spirit in those days,
    and they will prophesy.

¹⁹ I will show wonders in the heavens above
 and signs on the earth below,
 blood and fire and billows of smoke.
²⁰ The sun will be turned to darkness
 and the moon to blood
 before the coming of the great and glorious day of
the Lord.
²¹ And everyone who calls
 on the name of the Lord will be saved.'[c]

He explained how Jesus had fulfilled all Messianic prophecies from Abraham through Moses and how Jesus Christ died and was risen from the dead. It was the first preached full gospel sermon ever. The crowd listened. God had released the baptism of the Holy Spirit so that all true seekers of Messiah who gathered at Jerusalem could receive the message of the good news of salvation through Jesus Christ, and the gift of the baptism of the Holy Spirit. Many believers were from other nations, nations the gospel would reach as Jesus had promised.

Acts 1: ⁸ But you will receive power when the Holy Spirit comes on you; and you will be my witnesses in Jerusalem, and in all Judea and Samaria, and to the ends of the earth."

Peter preached all the major prophets and summarized how Jesus fulfilled the messianic prophecies. He also gave an altar call or got the crowd to make a decision for Christ. He didn't simply tell them, he preached to them they should repent, and receive the Holy Spirit. One of the main results of being baptised in the Holy Spirit is boldness to preach for Christ. It is a strong unction to tell others they can become Christians.

Acts 2; [36] "Therefore let all Israel be assured of this: God has made this Jesus, whom you crucified, both Lord and Messiah."
[37] When the people heard this, they were cut to the heart and said to Peter and the other apostles, "Brothers, what shall we do?"

[38] Peter replied, "Repent and be baptized, every one of you, in the name of Jesus Christ for the forgiveness of your sins. And you will receive the gift of the Holy Spirit. [39] The promise is for you and your children and for all who are far off—for all whom the Lord our God will call."

At this sermon about 3000 devout Jews gave their lives to Christ and were water baptized (into Jesus Christ) and baptized in the Holy Spirit. They gathered together each day in people's homes. They wanted to know more about Jesus, so they gathered together to learn from the disciples. There was multiplication in the church beyond what anyone could imagine. From 120 – 3000 in one day. Part of what they did is gather together each day.

Chapter 7 Study Questions

1. Are there coincidences? Or is there destiny or both? Describe in relation to the day of Pentecost and the Baptism of the Holy Spirit.

2. Describe your own life in terms of coincidence and destiny. What is your predominant view concerning people's lives?

3. How much is human will and how much is Divine destiny? Describe it in your life. Can Human will affect Divine destiny? Does Divine destiny affect human will?

4. The Church is multiethnic. The glory of the nations is in the multicultural multiethnic Church. Describe your own experiences with it and the importance of it in your own life and ministry.

8 THE FELLOWSHIP OF BELIEVERS

The Church gathered together regularly. It was each day at first. They cared for each others' needs. They met in small groups in people's homes. They shared their food, clothing etc. so that no one went without. They showed true love for each other. Be being together regularly, praying and learning about God, they grew closer and became knit together in their spirits. They trusted the Apostles with finances and giving to the poor.

Acts 2: [42] They devoted themselves to the apostles' teaching and to fellowship, to the breaking of bread and to prayer. [43] Everyone was filled with awe at the many wonders and signs performed by the apostles. [44] All the believers were together and had everything in common. [45] They sold property and possessions to give to anyone who had need. [46] Every day they continued to meet together in the temple courts. They broke bread in their homes and ate together with glad and sincere hearts, [47] praising God and enjoying the favor of all the people. And the Lord added to their number daily those who were being saved.

Acts 4: [32] All the believers were one in heart and mind. No one claimed that any of their possessions was their own, but they shared everything they had. [33] With great power the apostles continued to testify to the resurrection of the Lord Jesus. And

God's grace was so powerfully at work in them all[34] that there were no needy persons among them. For from time to time those who owned land or houses sold them, brought the money from the sales [35] and put it at the apostles' feet, and it was distributed to anyone who had need.

[36] Joseph, a Levite from Cyprus, whom the apostles called Barnabas (which means "son of encouragement"), [37] sold a field he owned and brought the money and put it at the apostles' feet.

Church Growth

The gifts of the Holy Spirit as well as the fruit of the Holy Spirit were evident in the lives of believers. The Holy Spirit would prompt them, and they would speak or pray or release miracles or healings with the gift of faith.

1 Corinthians 12: [7] Now to each one the manifestation of the Spirit is given for the common good. [8] To one there is given through the Spirit a message of wisdom, to another a message of knowledge by means of the same Spirit, [9] to another faith by the same Spirit, to another gifts of healing by that one Spirit, [10] to another miraculous powers, to another prophecy, to another distinguishing between spirits, to another speaking in different kinds of tongues,[a] and to still another the interpretation of tongues.[b] [11] All these are the work of

one and the same Spirit, and he distributes them to each one, just as he determines.

Galatians 5: [22] But the fruit of the Spirit is love, joy, peace, forbearance, kindness, goodness, faithfulness, [23] gentleness and self-control. Against such things there is no law.

The Gifts of the Holy Spirit

The gifts of Spirit were now resident in the believers. In the Old Testament, only prophets of God were moved upon by the Holy Spirit to prophesy or do miracles. The Holy Spirit would come upon a person and he or she would be used by God's Spirit. The baptism of the Holy Spirit is an immersion into Christ in such a way the Holy Spirit who comes to dwell in believers as they receive Christ, compels them from within. God's most Holy presence dwells within Christians. This is the Holy Spirit Jesus had promised. The nudging of the Holy Spirit, promptings of the Holy Spirit and unctions of the Holy Spirit compel Christians (from within their spirits) to be used of God. The result is always supernatural. The books of Acts is a record of many healings, deliverances, resurrections from the dead etc. God uses Christians who are willing to obey His promptings to bring salvation, healing, deliverance and other miracles into the earth.

There were miracles, healings and deliverance

Peter and John were ordinary men on their way to regular prayer in the temple. They were doing the normal but something supernatural occurred. In their regular lives of obedience to worship and pray, they encounter a man who could not walk. The Holy Spirit moved within the Apostle Peter and prompted him to the gifts of healing.

Acts 3: 1 One day Peter and John were going up to the temple at the time of prayer—at three in the afternoon. [2] Now a man who was lame from birth was being carried to the temple gate called Beautiful, where he was put every day to beg from those going into the temple courts. [3] When he saw Peter and John about to enter, he asked them for money. [4] Peter looked straight at him, as did John. Then Peter said, "Look at us!" [5] So the man gave them his attention, expecting to get something from them.

[6] Then Peter said, "Silver or gold I do not have, but what I do have I give you. In the name of Jesus Christ of Nazareth, walk." [7] Taking him by the right hand, he helped him up, and instantly the man's feet and ankles became strong. [8] He jumped to his feet and began to walk. Then he went with them into the temple courts, walking and jumping, and praising God. [9] When all the people saw him walking and praising God, [10] they recognized him as the same man who used to sit begging at the temple gate called Beautiful, and they were filled with wonder and amazement at what had happened to him.

The man who had never walked in his life and only knew begging as a life, suddenly was healed. His life was transformed. The news of healings and miracles spread the news of the followers of Jesus.

There was persecution from the Jewish leaders who saw them as a threat to their religion. Although there were healings and miracles, the religious people's hearts were rather hard rather than spiritual, so they were not open to the miracles as signs as God's love towards people. Rather than praise God for the miracle, the religious leaders fought against the disciples of Jesus and reprimanded them for doing miracles.

Acts 4: [18] Then they called them in again and commanded them not to speak or teach at all in the name of Jesus. [19] But Peter and John replied, "Which is right in God's eyes: to listen to you, or to him? You be the judges! [20] As for us, we cannot help speaking about what we have seen and heard."

[21] After further threats they let them go. They could not decide how to punish them, because all the people were praising God for what had happened. [22] For the man who was miraculously healed was over forty years old.

Peter and John knew that it was God who did the miracle and that they were obedient disciples of Christ or servants of God. There was no way they were not going to obey God and the Holy Spirit gave them boldness to proclaim it in spite of beatings, threats etc.

Acts 5: [17] Then the high priest and all his associates, who were members of the party of the Sadducees, were filled with jealousy. [18] They arrested the apostles and put them in the public jail. [19] But during the night an angel of the Lord opened the doors of the jail and brought them out. [20] "Go, stand in the temple courts," he said, "and tell the people all about this new life."

[21] At daybreak they entered the temple courts, as they had been told, and began to teach the people.

Angelic visitations occurred. An angel got them out of prison. They were miraculously released. The Holy Spirit was manifesting special miracles in the lives of the disciples.

When the high priest and his associates arrived, they called together the Sanhedrin—the full assembly of the elders of Israel—and sent to the jail for the apostles. [22] But on arriving at the jail, the officers did not find them there. So they went back and reported, [23] "We found the jail securely locked, with the guards standing at the doors; but when we opened them, we found no one inside." [24] On hearing this report, the captain of the temple guard and the chief priests were at a loss, wondering what this might lead to.

Other occasions, the apostles were physically beaten, put in prison but they continued teaching and preaching Christ. The baptism of the Holy Spirit gave them boldness to preach. The books of Acts is a record of beatings, martyrs, boldness and manifestations of healings and miracles in the new Church.

Acts 5: ⁴¹ The apostles left the Sanhedrin, rejoicing because they had been counted worthy of suffering disgrace for the Name. ⁴² Day after day, in the temple courts and from house to house, they never stopped teaching and proclaiming the good news that Jesus is the Messiah.

The first deacons were appointed in Jerusalem because the church had grown so large that the apostles couldn't help every one without extra help. They prayed and chose spiritual men with the gifts of the spirit also with godly lives or the fruit of the spirit to be the first deacons. They would help serve widows and orphans and some of the physical service ministry to the poor. The Apostles could continue to teach and preach the things of Jesus. The servants chosen were spiritually gifted. They were honourable. They were anointed or showed the presence of God in their lives. Being a servant in the church is an important ministry and the criteria for choosing servants is clearly shown by the Apostles in their decision making.

Acts 6: ²So the Twelve gathered all the disciples together and said, "It would not be right for us to neglect the ministry of the word of God in order to wait on tables. ³Brothers and sisters, choose seven men from among you who are known to be full of the Spirit and wisdom. We will turn this responsibility over to them ⁴and will give our attention to prayer and the ministry of the word."

⁵This proposal pleased the whole group. They chose Stephen, a man full of faith and of the Holy Spirit; also Philip, Procorus, Nicanor, Timon, Parmenas, and Nicolas from Antioch, a convert to Judaism. ⁶They presented these men to the apostles, who prayed and laid their hands on them.

⁷So the word of God spread. The number of disciples in Jerusalem increased rapidly, and a large number of priests became obedient to the faith.

The disciple Stephen preached, served and was stoned to death because of his Christian faith. He was a passionate follower of Jesus and rather than not speak, he preached the prophets and the prophecies the Messiah fulfilled. He preached Jesus to the religious Jews who hated him. Even as they hurled stones to throw at him, he prayed forgiving them and committing his spirit to God. It was the Holy Spirit that gave Stephan boldness. It was the Holy Spirit that empowered him to continue strongly until the death.

Acts 7: 54 When the members of the Sanhedrin heard this, they were furious and gnashed their teeth at him. 55 But Stephen, full of the Holy Spirit, looked up to heaven and saw the glory of God, and Jesus standing at the right hand of God. 56 "Look," he said, "I see heaven open and the Son of Man standing at the right hand of God."

57 At this they covered their ears and, yelling at the top of their voices, they all rushed at him, 58 dragged him out of the city and began to stone him. Meanwhile, the witnesses laid their coats at the feet of a young man named Saul.

Opposition to the gospel

Although there were miracles, the religious Jews persecuted the Christians. It became so severe that the Christians were scattered because of opposition against them. They went to other regions surrounding Jerusalem and preached Jesus Christ there. The opposition is horrible, but the result was that the Christians continued preaching and teaching Christ in other areas.

Acts 8: 1 On that day a great persecution broke out against the church in Jerusalem, and all except the apostles were scattered throughout Judea and Samaria. 2 Godly men buried Stephen and mourned deeply for him. 3 But Saul began to destroy the church. Going from house to house, he dragged off both men and women and put them in prison.

The Jerusalem Church was scattered

The disciples were led by the Holy Spirit and the gifts of the Spirit were manifest in the church in all the communities they were in. They were scattered but it meant the gospel was reaching more places than simply Jerusalem.

Acts 1: [8]But you will receive power when the Holy Spirit comes on you; and you will be my witnesses in Jerusalem, and in all Judea and Samaria, and to the ends of the earth."

The disciple Philip lead a revival in the city of Samaria. There was preaching, healings and miracles evident. There was a strong presence of the Holy Spirit and the evidence of it. Philip was obedient to God. Rather than stay in Samaria, he obeyed the prompting of the Holy Spirit and it led to a pilgrim from Ethiopia becoming a Christian.

Evangelism

Acts 8: [4]Those who had been scattered preached the word wherever they went.[5]Philip went down to a city in Samaria and proclaimed the Messiah there. [6]When the crowds heard Philip and saw the signs he performed, they all paid close attention to what he said. [7]For with shrieks, impure spirits came out of many, and many who were paralyzed, or lame were healed. ⁸ So there was great joy in that city.

The disciple Philip obeyed the Holy Spirit and helped to impact the nation of Ethiopia. The Holy Spirit arranged for Philip to encounter a true seeker of God who was studying the scriptures of the Messiah but didn't understand them. At that exact moment, Philip started preaching to Him the Messiah Jesus. The Ethiopian Eunuch immediately received the word of salvation and accepted Jesus. He was baptized and filled with the Holy Spirit. Obedience to the promptings of the Holy Spirit – the gifts of the Spirit as well as knowledge of the scriptures was necessary and vital to the multiplication of the Church.

Acts 8: ²⁶ Now an angel of the Lord said to Philip, "Go south to the road—the desert road—that goes down from Jerusalem to Gaza." ²⁷ So he started out, and on his way he met an Ethiopian[a] eunuch, an important official in charge of all the treasury of the Kandace (which means "queen of the Ethiopians"). This man had gone to Jerusalem to worship, ²⁸ and on his way home was sitting in his chariot reading the Book of Isaiah the prophet. ²⁹ The Spirit told Philip, "Go to that chariot and stay near it."

³⁰ Then Philip ran up to the chariot and heard the man reading Isaiah the prophet. "Do you understand what you are reading?" Philip asked.

[31] "How can I," he said, "unless someone explains it to me?" So he invited Philip to come up and sit with him.

[32] This is the passage of Scripture the eunuch was reading:

"He was led like a sheep to the slaughter,
    and as a lamb before its shearer is silent,
    so he did not open his mouth.
[33] In his humiliation he was deprived of justice.
    Who can speak of his descendants?
    For his life was taken from the earth."[b]
[34] The eunuch asked Philip, "Tell me, please, who is the prophet talking about, himself or someone else?" [35] Then Philip began with that very passage of Scripture and told him the good news about Jesus.

[36] As they traveled along the road, they came to some water and the eunuch said, "Look, here is water. What can stand in the way of my being baptized?" [37][c] [38] And he gave orders to stop the chariot. Then both Philip and the eunuch went down into the water and Philip baptized him. [39] When they came up out of the water, the Spirit of the Lord suddenly took Philip away, and the eunuch did not see him again, but went on his way rejoicing. [40] Philip, however, appeared at Azotus and traveled about, preaching the gospel in all the towns until he reached Caesarea.

The Holy Spirit led Philip to the person searching to know more about God. The Holy Spirit gave Philip the words to speak to the Eunuch. Although a regular human, Philip with the indwelling Holy Spirit was an evangelist to the nations; he preaches Jesus as Messiah and baptism by water and spirit. The Eunuch receives all of it because he was sincerely seeking God. A miracle occurs after the Eunuch is baptized, Philip is translated. This means that although he was physically present with the Eunuch, suddenly the Holy Spirit translated him or moved him to a different spot. It is a miracle that occurs. His body is transported to a different place.

The Church of Jesus Christ was reaching beyond Jerusalem and now had been entrusted to Ethiopia through the Eunuch. The Church was not to only be a local gathering in Jerusalem but to spread through all the earth. God used the Apostles, disciples and others to do it. A center for missions was established by the most unlikely person, in Antioch.

Chapter 8 Study Questions

1. Describe your interpretation of the Antioch church and its similarity or differences from this chapter.
2. Describe the different ministry gifts of the five-fold ministry gifts who have ministered in your

life. List at least one for each. Describe how each imparted you directly.

3. In your pursuit of ministry how do you plan to connect with the other five-fold ministry gifts?

9 THE ANTIOCH CHURCH: A MODEL OF THE NEW TESTAMENT CHURCH

Although the Church at Jerusalem remained (even though many disciples scattered) the disciples at Jerusalem hid secretly and preached and taught privately to avoid death.

The Antioch Church – was founded by The Apostle Paul and Barnabas in a Gentile region where people received the message of Christ Jesus gladly and they had much freedom of worship and gathering. There was coming, going, planting, revisiting, establishing, part always fluid, part always changing as people come and go bringing life, encouragement etc. It began by the disciple Barnabas going to Saul and encouraging him to come preach with him. They went as missionaries to Antioch. They planted a church and it was there the term Christian or Christ follower was used.

Acts 11: [25] Then Barnabas went to Tarsus to look for Saul, [26] and when he found him, he brought him to Antioch. So for a whole year Barnabas and Saul met with the church and taught great numbers of people. The disciples were called Christians first at Antioch.

Saul of Tarsus

Saul of Tarsus was an unlikely candidate to become a Christian. He was not a follower of Jesus. He was of the religious Jews who opposed Christians. Saul of Tarsus was a man who was well educated, a Pharisee of Pharisees. He was a teacher and well-respected member of the Religious rulers of Jerusalem. He was zealous, passionate, and believed as did the other religious Jews that Christians were their enemies because they believed it was a false religion. He took it upon himself to fight against them. He wrote letters to arrest Christians and saw to their deaths. The church knew of him because of his reputation. Saul of Tarsus was going about his regular activity of rounding up Christians, when he encountered God. It was not a person who preached Jesus Christ to him, but God Himself appeared to Him in a miraculous way.

A bright light appeared, and he was thrown to the ground and blinded by the bright light. He heard the voice of Jesus, and His response was "Who are you, LORD?" Saul did not recognize the voice. He did not know Jesus was God until the next phrase. "I am Jesus."

Immediately Saul became a Christian. He knew he had encountered God. He was blinded. He couldn't see. He heard the voice of God instructing him to go to

Jerusalem, so God could give him instruction. He obeyed. His life was immediately changed. He become a passionate Christian. All the passion he had in hating Christians became compassion for those who did not know Jesus. He obeyed the instructions and in Jerusalem a Christian, Ananias, was praying and God spoke to him to go pray for Saul become Paul so that he may be healed.

Apostle Paul – Acts 9: 1 Meanwhile, Saul was still breathing out murderous threats against the Lord's disciples. He went to the high priest 2 and asked him for letters to the synagogues in Damascus, so that if he found any there who belonged to the Way, whether men or women, he might take them as prisoners to Jerusalem. 3 As he neared Damascus on his journey, suddenly a light from heaven flashed around him. 4 He fell to the ground and heard a voice say to him, "Saul, Saul, why do you persecute me?"

5 "Who are you, Lord?" Saul asked.

"I am Jesus, whom you are persecuting," he replied. 6 "Now get up and go into the city, and you will be told what you must do."

Saul obeyed God. He went to Jerusalem and although physically blind, he waited for God's messenger to come pray for his healing.

Ananias comes

Ananias was praying, and in the midst of his prayers God instructed him to go pray for Saul of Tarsus, so he could be healed. At first Ananias tried to resist the instruction because of the horrible reputation of Saul, but God gives him direct instruction and specific instruction. It was a divine connection. Ananias obeyed God and Saul was at the exact place God directed him to. Saul was blind, and Ananias welcomed him into the body of Christ as he prayed and touched him, Saul was healed. God sent a mature Christian to minister to Saul. With Saul's healing, he immediately began teaching and preaching Christ.

Acts 9: [15] But the Lord said to Ananias, "Go! This man is my chosen instrument to proclaim my name to the Gentiles and their kings and to the people of Israel. [16] I will show him how much he must suffer for my name."

[17] Then Ananias went to the house and entered it. Placing his hands on Saul, he said, "Brother Saul, the Lord—Jesus, who appeared to you on the road as you were coming here—has sent me so that you may see again and be filled with the Holy Spirit." [18] Immediately, something like scales fell from Saul's eyes, and he could see again. He got up and was baptized, [19] and after taking some food, he regained his strength.

The disciple Ananias obedience to Christ can not be over emphasized in its importance. Because Ananias obeyed God, Saul was healed, and a connection was made that was supernatural. Apostle Paul was radically transformed and immediately began preaching Christ in places he once persecuted the Christians. Many did not believe until Paul was to be arrested for preaching Jesus by the Jewish leaders.

Acts 9: 23 After many days had gone by, there was a conspiracy among the Jews to kill him, 24 but Saul learned of their plan. Day and night they kept close watch on the city gates in order to kill him. 25 But his followers took him by night and lowered him in a basket through an opening in the wall.

Raised and educated as a Pharisee. Passionate against Christians – suddenly become a zealous Christian agent for Christ. He immediately tried to connect with the Apostles because they were the Church leaders at Jerusalem and because they had known Jesus personally. He wanted to learn from them. Of course, they were suspicious because of his murdering reputation. Finally, Barnabas (his name is son of consolation) met with him and brought him to the other disciples in Jerusalem.

Acts 9: 26 When he came to Jerusalem, he tried to join the disciples, but they were all afraid of him, not believing that he really was a disciple. 27 But Barnabas took him and brought him to the apostles.

He told them how Saul on his journey had seen the Lord and that the Lord had spoken to him, and how in Damascus he had preached fearlessly in the name of Jesus. [28] So Saul stayed with them and moved about freely in Jerusalem, speaking boldly in the name of the Lord. [29] He talked and debated with the Hellenistic Jews,[a] but they tried to kill him. [30] When the believers learned of this, they took him down to Caesarea and sent him off to Tarsus.

Paul continued teaching and preaching, earning his own living in Tarsus. There he worked and preached until the disciple Barnabas came and compelled him to go on a missionary journey with him to Antioch. (Acts 11: 25)

The Apostle Peter

The Apostle Peter was praying on his roof when he had a revelation from God that the message of Jesus salvation was not for Jews alone but also for Gentiles. (Acts 10). God showed him a vision of all sorts of forbidden animals. They were forbidden in the Old covenant with Moses. God was telling him to partake of them and he rejected it saying it was unclean because that is what was taught in the covenant with Moses. God spoke and said He was not to reject what God had cleansed.

He knew that it was God speaking to him in the vision because immediately there were gentiles at the door wanting to speak with him. In the covenant with Moses, Gentiles were not welcome except as slaves because they worshipped other gods. But Peter knew that the message he received from God was to show him that the gentiles could become Christians. He went to the home of Cornelius, a centurion (a Roman believer in God), and lead him and all with him to the saving knowledge of Jesus Christ. They were all baptized in water and filled with the Holy Spirit speaking in other tongues. Peter shared this truth with the disciples. Jesus Christ was also for the gentiles. This was a radical change because the Jews and the gentiles were so different and in the covenant with Moses, they were as slaves or not equal because of their false gods.

Acts 11: 4Starting from the beginning, Peter told them the whole story: 5"I was in the city of Joppa praying, and in a trance I saw a vision. I saw something like a large sheet being let down from heaven by its four corners, and it came down to where I was. 6I looked into it and saw four-footed animals of the earth, wild beasts, reptiles and birds. 7Then I heard a voice telling me, 'Get up, Peter. Kill and eat.'

8"I replied, 'Surely not, Lord! Nothing impure or unclean has ever entered my mouth.'

9"The voice spoke from heaven a second time, 'Do not call anything impure that God has made clean.' [10]This happened three times, and then it was all pulled up to heaven again.

[11]"Right then three men who had been sent to me from Caesarea stopped at the house where I was staying. [12]The Spirit told me to have no hesitation about going with them. These six brothers also went with me, and we entered the man's house. [13]He told us how he had seen an angel appear in his house and say, 'Send to Joppa for Simon who is called Peter. [14]He will bring you a message through which you and all your household will be saved.'

[15]"As I began to speak, the Holy Spirit came on them as he had come on us at the beginning. [16]Then I remembered what the Lord had said: 'John baptized with[a] water, but you will be baptized with[b] the Holy Spirit.'[17]So if God gave them the same gift he gave us who believed in the Lord Jesus Christ, who was I to think that I could stand in God's way?"

[18]When they heard this, they had no further objections and praised God, saying, "So then, even to Gentiles God has granted repentance that leads to life."

Acts 11: [5]"As I began to speak, the Holy Spirit came on them as he had come on us at the beginning. [16]Then I remembered what the Lord had said: 'John baptized with[a] water, but you will be baptized with[b] the Holy Spirit.'[17]So if God gave them the same gift he gave us who believed in the Lord

Jesus Christ, who was I to think that I could stand in God's way?"

18 When they heard this, they had no further objections and praised God, saying, "So then, even to Gentiles God has granted repentance that leads to life."

Peter's revelation of salvation for all people c hanged his life. Peter became a missionary visiting the churches planted by the Apostle Paul. He was a part of the foundation of the Church at Jerusalem and taught and preached to both Jews and Gentiles.

Chapter 9 Study Questions

1. Describe the importance of your spouse in ministry. If not married, imagine it in your future.
2. Is it necessary for the spouse to be involved in ministry for a successful marriage as well as ministry?
3. There are often teams of people – not only spouses- that God calls into ministry together for a purpose. List the people you can count on to assist you with ministry. How will you recruit more?
4. Describe your relationship discipling others. List at least 1 or 2 and describe it. If you cannot, please consider what you can do to begin. What person can you begin sharing the

things of God with so he or she will train up others?

10 ANTIOCH WAS A MISSION'S BASE

Acts 12: 25 When Barnabas and Saul had finished their mission, they returned from[a] Jerusalem, taking with them John, also called Mark.

There were evangelists, pastors, prophets, apostles and teachers at Antioch. There were people coming with refreshing news of the miracles God was doing and there was connection with the Jerusalem Church. It was a main connection point for Christians because of the liberty they had to worship God freely there.

First fruits of the Gentiles

The Church planted was the first major Christian church besides Jerusalem. Jesus had spoken to his disciples that there would be gentiles, Greeks, who would come to know him, but he spoke it in such a way they did not comprehend it. As Jesus was preaching in Jerusalem before his arrest and his death, Philip came to tell Jesus there were Greeks who were interested in becoming believers. Jesus was trying to tell Philip that it was not the season of the Gentiles. He explained it in a parable. "The son of man dying" was Jesus giving his life for us so that anyone who believed could become a Christian. He was the single seed that was placed in the earth becoming many. By his death, burial and resurrection, anyone who would believe in Jesus could be saved. The resurrection of Jesus from the dead was the first hope for all Gentiles. The baptism of the Holy Spirit of the Apostles during Pentecost was the first releasing of the truths of Christ to the nations. The Church at Antioch was the first fruits of the Gentiles. The multiplication of the gospel of Jesus Christ to the Gentiles. It is a direct fulfillment of the prophecy of Jesus.

John 12: 20 Now there were some Greeks among those who went up to worship at the festival. 21 They came to Philip, who was from Bethsaida in Galilee, with a request. "Sir," they said, "we would like to see Jesus." 22 Philip went to tell Andrew; Andrew and Philip in turn told Jesus.

23 Jesus replied, "The hour has come for the Son of Man to be glorified. 24 Very truly I tell you, unless a kernel of wheat falls to the ground and dies, it remains only a single seed. But if it dies, it produces many seeds. 25 Anyone who loves their life will lose it, while anyone who hates their life in this world will keep it for eternal life. 26 Whoever serves me must follow me; and where I am, my servant also will be. My Father will honor the one who serves me.

Antioch

Antioch was a center for the building up the church for the equipping of the saints for the work of the ministry. It was a training and equipping center. All the ministry gifts were present. There were core aspects of it that made it unique and a model for our new testament churches. There were Apostles, prophets, evangelists, pastors and teachers. The variety of Giftings was used to build up the church.

Ephesians 4: [11] So Christ himself gave the apostles, the prophets, the evangelists, the pastors and teachers, [12] to equip his people for works of service, so that the body of Christ may be built up [13] until we all reach unity in the faith and in the knowledge of the Son of God and become mature, attaining to the whole measure of the fullness of Christ.

Chapter 10 Study questions

1. Describe a goal for yourself in ministry with a missions' base. How important will it be to you? Is there a church now that you attend that will be it? Is there a Church you would like to be a part of that could be it?
2. Compare your local church to a missions' base. How often are people being welcomed as new members? How often are people being commissioned and released for ministry? Describe at least one of each.
3. Involving all ages of people in ministry activities is important. In your ministry goal how will you involve as many ages of Christians as possible?

What target audience will you be mostly reaching?

11 THE MINISTRY GIFTS

The ministry gifts are special gifts to the Church. They are all essential in the "perfecting of the saints" for the work of the ministry. They work together to equip, train and launch other Christians in their giftings and talents. They are all necessary, so there should be a regular input from all of the ministry gifts into a congregation. The Antioch Church was a headquarters for all the ministry gifts in missionary exploits.

Pastors

Pastors usually preach or teach in one congregation for long durations. Some pastors stay for all their lives. They shepherd the sheep. They teach the covenants of God (Adam, Noah, Abraham, Moses) as well as administer the sacraments of God (water baptism, baby dedication, baptism of the Holy Spirit, foot washing, communion, anointing with oil, marriage). They also preach salvation, pray with people, conduct church services and funerals. Usually their main gifts are in leadership and teaching.

There are different types of pastors depending on their giftings. God gives the giftings as He wills. Some pastors preach expository teaching that is thorough, in depth and essential for the church to receive spiritual life. They prepare their messages through studying scripture, emphasizing the logos, (God's written word) using commentaries and other Biblical helps. Sometimes there is reference to Hebrew or Greeks meanings for more explanation. It is excellent when it is combined with prayer and spoken by God's pastor who speaks by inspiration as well as according to his or her outline or sermon notes. A good teaching sermon can touch the hearts of the new believers as well as the seasoned saints. It compels those who don't know Christ to want to know Him.

A prophetic Pastor will often speak in the direct unction from the Holy Spirit the RHEMA word of God. The quickened word of God, or the inspired scriptures. God will give them a quickening of scripture and they will prepare their sermons around that passage or passages of scripture. It is thorough, balanced but also directly aimed at the congregation it is prepared for. It is God's word to those people at that season. The result is often the whole congregation responding to an altar call and a life changing message brought to the people. Often the pastor will flow in the gifts of the Spirit as he or she ministers and words of wisdom, words of knowledge, discerning of spirits will occur. Also, there may be miracles or healings manifest.

Teachers

Although most pastors are teachers, not all teachers are pastors. Some study the scriptures and prepare lessons for children, youth, or adults. They study using the resources of scripture and Biblical aids, but they specialize in the groups they are speaking to. Often, they are not known by all the others in the church unless they were taught by them. Their knowledge of scripture is essential, so a novice or new believer should not become a teacher. The new Christians can serve elsewhere but not as teachers. The main aspects of our Bible are taught through teachers.

Evangelists

Evangelists are passionate about souls. They will often receive special direction from God personally by experiencing a divine healing or dream or vision of people who must come to Christ or go to hell. Compassion will overwhelm them for those who must come to Christ and they will dedicate their lives to serving God by travelling preaching and teaching. Some travel within their region. Some travel to other nations. All of them sacrifice their normal lives so that others can come to know Christ. Mostly, they travel and preach.

Some are world famous and some are not. Their main focus is preaching salvation, healing and deliverance through Jesus Christ. Often miracles and healings occur through their ministry.

Apostles

The Apostles did not end with the 12 disciples who knew Jesus on earth. The Apostle Paul came not knowing Jesus as a human but encountering him supernaturally. Most Apostles are supernaturally visited by Jesus in a dream, vision or some other way. They encounter Jesus and it causes them to want to bring the gospel to all the nations. They are foundations of the church. They plant Churches. They plant Christian ministries. They plant Bible Colleges and other huge projects. They often operate in all the gifts of the Spirit and can train up any member of the ministry team. They are not usually in once place. They have a home base, but their main function is to plant churches and train up ministers of the gospel. The anointing on them is so strong that usually supernatural manifestations of the gifts of healing, working of miracles and gift of faith are evident through their ministry. Some are appointed over regions; some are appointed to a nation; some are appointed to the nations. God is the one who gives the gifts.

A person who wears a nametag that says Apostle does not make him an Apostle. They are proven ministers of God. Their fruit is the churches they plant, and the people's lives they have transformed by the preaching of the gospel.

Prophets

Prophets usually are using their spiritual gifts of tongues, interpretation of tongues and prophecy in the congregations they serve in. They bring words of encouragement, exhortation and comfort. They are encouragers. Those with the office of prophet (proven by ministry) also give warnings and speak the truth whether or not people are cheering them on. Many of the prophets in the Scriptures had tough lives because they spoke God's Words to the people, but the people didn't receive them. Prophets are the mouthpiece of God. They speak what God prompts them to speak. A true prophet will always speak things that are in line with scripture. They will never speak words that contradict God's Word.

They are visionaries also who preach what God wants to do such as Isaiah who preached God's ultimate plan was to receive Israel back as His people even though there was a period when Israel was not following God.

Antioch Church Acts 15: [30] So the men were sent off and went down to Antioch, where they gathered the church together and delivered the letter. [31] The people read it and were glad for its encouraging message. [32] Judas and Silas, who themselves were prophets, said much to encourage and strengthen the believers. [33] After spending some time there, they were sent off by the believers with the blessing of peace to return to those who had sent them. [34] [d] [35] But Paul and Barnabas remained in Antioch, where they and many others taught and preached the word of the Lord.

Prophets and Apostles were regularly coming. The prophets released Paul; and Barnabas as ministers and launched them onto missions' ministry with prayer and prophesy. Teaching and preaching – various letters and books of Bible by the authors. Witnesses of Jesus – imparting to those who did not know him. It was first fruits of the Gentiles

Acts 13: [1] Now in the church at Antioch there were prophets and teachers: Barnabas, Simeon called Niger, Lucius of Cyrene, Manaen (who had been brought up with Herod the tetrarch) and Saul. [2] While they were worshiping the Lord and fasting, the Holy Spirit said, "Set apart for me Barnabas and Saul for the work to which I have called them." [3] So after they had fasted and prayed, they placed their hands on them and sent them off.

The Gentiles were open to hearing about Jesus. They worshipped many idols but listened to the teaching and the preaching of the disciples. Not all received Christ, but some did. They preached in synagogues at first. Some of the Jews received. Once Jews totally rejected the message – the apostle Paul devoted his preaching to missions alone. They planted churches in homes of people. They revisited the people to encourage them and build them up strengthen them.

Acts 13: 4 The two of them, sent on their way by the Holy Spirit, went down to Seleucia and sailed from there to Cyprus. 5 When they arrived at Salamis, they proclaimed the word of God in the Jewish synagogues. John was with them as their helper.

6 They traveled through the whole island until they came to Paphos. There they met a Jewish sorcerer and false prophet named Bar-Jesus, 7 who was an attendant of the proconsul, Sergius Paulus. The proconsul, an intelligent man, sent for Barnabas and Saul because he wanted to hear the word of God.

The gospel message is the message of Jesus The Messiah

This message was first preached to the Jews but also to the Gentiles. This fulfilling Jesus' words in Acts 1: 7 He said to them: "It is not for you to know the times or dates the Father has set by his own authority. [8] But you will receive power when the Holy Spirit comes on you; and you will be my witnesses in Jerusalem, and in all Judea and Samaria, and to the ends of the earth."

Paul and Barnabas preached Jesus Christ by explaining how Jesus fulfilled all the Messianic prophecies. They referred to scriptures comparing the covenant with Moses to the New Testament of Jesus shed blood.

Acts 13: [38] "Therefore, my friends, I want you to know that through Jesus the forgiveness of sins is proclaimed to you. [39] Through him everyone who believes is set free from every sin, a justification you were not able to obtain under the law of Moses.

[42] As Paul and Barnabas were leaving the synagogue, the people invited them to speak further about these things on the next Sabbath. [43] When the congregation was dismissed, many of the Jews and devout converts to Judaism followed Paul and Barnabas, who talked with them and urged them to continue in the grace of God.

There was controversy – they brought a message dividing the Old religious people from those who would receive Christ. The Word of God divides soul from spirit (Hebrews 4:12). The preaching of the gospel divides people. Some quickly turn to Christ; others are hardened against it.

Acts 14:1 At Iconium Paul and Barnabas went as usual into the Jewish synagogue. There they spoke so effectively that a great number of Jews and Greeks believed. ²But the Jews who refused to believe stirred up the other Gentiles and poisoned their minds against the brothers. ³So Paul and Barnabas spent considerable time there, speaking boldly for the Lord, who confirmed the message of his grace by enabling them to perform signs and wonders. ⁴The people of the city were divided; some sided with the Jews, others with the apostles. ⁵There was a plot afoot among both Gentiles and Jews, together with their leaders, to mistreat them and stone them. ⁶But they found out about it and fled to the Lycaonian cities of Lystra and Derbe and to the surrounding country,⁷where they continued to preach the gospel.

God's Word divides flesh from spirit. God's word penetrates the inner most being of a person.

Hebrews 4: ¹²For the word of God is alive and active. Sharper than any double-edged sword, it penetrates even to dividing soul and spirit, joints and marrow; it judges the thoughts and attitudes of the heart. ¹³Nothing in all creation is hidden from God's sight.

Miracles

The Antioch Church had all the gifts of the Spirit and manifestations of God's glory such as people getting saved, healed and receiving miracles. These miracles were evidence to unbelievers who immediately believed but in their ignorance were instructed not to worship the Apostles but God. The Gentiles had many gods, so the miracles immediately reached them. They were open to receive teaching from the Apostles. The Apostles instructed them bringing the truths of God's covenants as well as the truth of the Triune God.

Acts 14: [8]In Lystra there sat a man who was lame. He had been that way from birth and had never walked. [9]He listened to Paul as he was speaking. Paul looked directly at him, saw that he had faith to be healed [10]and called out, "Stand up on your feet!" At that, the man jumped up and began to walk.

[11]When the crowd saw what Paul had done, they shouted in the Lycaonian language, "The gods have come down to us in human form!"[12]Barnabas they called Zeus, and Paul they called Hermes because he was the chief speaker. [13]The priest of Zeus, whose temple was just outside the city, brought bulls and wreaths to the city gates because he and the crowd wanted to offer sacrifices to them.

¹⁴ But when the apostles Barnabas and Paul heard of this, they tore their clothes and rushed out into the crowd, shouting: ¹⁵ "Friends, why are you doing this? We too are only human, like you. We are bringing you good news, telling you to turn from these worthless things to the living God, who made the heavens and the earth and the sea and everything in them. ¹⁶ In the past, he let all nations go their own way. ¹⁷ Yet he has not left himself without testimony: He has shown kindness by giving you rain from heaven and crops in their seasons; he provides you with plenty of food and fills your hearts with joy." ¹⁸ Even with these words, they had difficulty keeping the crowd from sacrificing to them.

Base

Antioch was a missions' base church – The apostles would return there to strengthen the disciples bringing refreshing news of what God was doing in other parts of the world. Their excitement brought refreshing continuously to the church. It was a centre of teaching the doctrines of Christ as well as the truths of the covenants of Abraham and Moses. The only Bible they had was the Torah and letters being written by disciples that they copied and shared with each other on living a Christian life. They taught the scriptures and made disciples.

Acts 14: [21] They preached the gospel in that city and won a large number of disciples. Then they returned to Lystra, Iconium and Antioch, [22] strengthening the disciples and encouraging them to remain true to the faith. "We must go through many hardships to enter the kingdom of God," they said. [23] Paul and Barnabas appointed elders[a] for them in each church and, with prayer and fasting, committed them to the Lord, in whom they had put their trust.

Acts 14: [26] From Attalia they sailed back to Antioch, where they had been committed to the grace of God for the work they had now completed. [27] On arriving there, they gathered the church together and reported all that God had done through them and how he had opened a door of faith to the Gentiles. [28] And they stayed there a long time with the disciples.

The salvation of the Gentiles brought controversy to the church in Jerusalem because some wanted the Gentiles to become Jews first. It meant physical circumcision and well as keeping all the Levitical laws. After hearing the testimony of Paul, of the acceptance of Jesus as Messiah and them becoming baptized in water and in the Holy Spirit, sending Peter to visit the churches planted by Paul, the Council at Jerusalem after much discussion and much prayer released a document with their conclusion. Jerusalem – the home church of most of the apostles, remained the main authorized church.

The main point to the writing is that the only requirements of the new gentile believers was that they abstain from sexual immorality and they not consume blood.

The Council's Letter to Gentile Believers

Acts 15: ²²Then the apostles and elders, with the whole church, decided to choose some of their own men and send them to Antioch with Paul and Barnabas. They chose Judas (called Barsabbas) and Silas, men who were leaders among the believers. ²³With them they sent the following letter:

The apostles and elders, your brothers,

To the Gentile believers in Antioch, Syria and Cilicia:

Greetings.

²⁴We have heard that some went out from us without our authorization and disturbed you, troubling your minds by what they said. ²⁵So we all agreed to choose some men and send them to you with our dear friends Barnabas and Paul— ²⁶men who have risked their lives for the name of our Lord Jesus Christ. ²⁷Therefore we are sending Judas and Silas to confirm by word of mouth what we are writing. ²⁸It seemed good to the Holy Spirit and to us not to burden you with anything beyond the following requirements: ²⁹You are to abstain from food

---

sacrificed to idols, from blood, from the meat of strangled animals and from sexual immorality. You will do well to avoid these things.

Farewell.

The letter is quite radical because it does not demand that new Christians become Jews first. The issue is resolved at Jerusalem by The Apostles themselves. It is important because it is resolved by the church elders who resolve any issues that any Jewish believers in Christ might have regarding the new Gentile believers in Christ.

Galatians 3: [26] So in Christ Jesus you are all children of God through faith, [27] for all of you who were baptized into Christ have clothed yourselves with Christ.[28] There is neither Jew nor Gentile, neither slave nor free, nor is there male and female, for you are all one in Christ Jesus. [29] If you belong to Christ, then you are Abraham's seed, and heirs according to the promise.

The Jewish believers continued celebrating the Jewish feasts and keeping the Sabbath. The Gentile believers were taught by the Apostles, so I am sure they celebrated the feasts etc.

Although not obliged to keep the feasts or other Levitical laws, there is value in celebrating them to those Christians who want to partake of the blessings of them as each of those feasts is for a specific purpose. The topic is worthy of in-depth study beyond the emphasis of this book. There has been since the 1990's in North America, more and more Christian churches celebrating some or all of the feasts. I myself have taken part in some of them and the teaching is always Christ centered. Robin Samson has an excellent book on the Jewish feasts from a Messianic perspective. It has excellent helps to aid parents in schooling their children as well as in depth study with research with a thorough Bibliography of other resources.

The Church at Antioch had a fluid quality to it. It was always welcoming people in and commissioning people for ministry. There was church growth. There was constant life with missionaries giving testimonies, Apostles giving teaching etc. This is essential to any Christian Church. There should always be people coming in with exciting news of missions. There should be people trained and equipped for ministry. They should be anointed, prayed over, launched or sent by the church for evangelism or missionary work planting other churches. Evangelists and missionaries are necessary to church growth as well as stimulation or refreshing. In Ezekiel, an angel guides the prophet to a river so beautiful – it flows from the throne of God. On both sides of the river trees flourish bearing much fruit, but there is one area that is not fruitful.

Ez 47: [11] But the swamps and marshes will not become fresh; they will be left for salt.

The swamps and the marshes are areas where there is no movement of water. The water is stagnant and not life giving. The way to prevent our churches from becoming this way is constant connection with the other parts of the ministry gifts. Especially missionaries or evangelists who come and report what God is doing, as well as Apostles and prophets who commission people to go plant churches or bring the news of Christ to people in other parts of the community. Always keep a life line in missions and evangelism and the church will continue to grow.

The river in Ezekiel is the Holy Spirit. It flows from the throne of God. It is life giving. It is fruitful. There are fish; there are fruit trees along side of it. It is a life-giving river. The Holy Spirit's presence in the church expressed through true worship and praise, the gifts of the Spirit manifest in the church and spiritual fruit in the lives of the members of the church make all the difference.

The Holy Spirit

People who know their spiritual gifts and use them freely in church gatherings, will develop them. It is the Holy Spirit, God Himself ministering through the church, to the church the life of God. An indicator of church life is the presence of The Holy Spirit in the church. Rather than squeeze in some praise and worship, we should be gathering to soak in the presence of God. Rather than rush to the next item on the church program agenda, we should wait to see the direction the Holy Spirit wants to move. There should always be tongues, interpretation of tongues and prophecy in our congregational services. The absence of it is a sign of religion.

Religion is a man-made attempt to please God. Allowing the Holy Spirit to direct the service is obeying the promptings of the Holy Spirit to praise, worship, prophesy, lead altar calls, pray etc. Of course, the pastors or elders must ultimately be responsible for this as it is their position to discern and lead the services. Should the pastor be discerning and go with the moving of the Holy Spirit, all the church will follow, and it will bring refreshing and sometimes healing or other miracles in the church.

1 Corinthians 14: [39] Therefore, my brothers and sisters, be eager to prophesy, and do not forbid speaking in tongues. [40] But everything should be done in a fitting and orderly way.

The Holy Spirit

Following the promptings of the Holy Spirit will result in the beauty of Christ shining through His Church. There may be some weeping. There may be some laughing. There may be some dancing or jumping. There may be a Jericho march around the church. If it is not of the spirit it is nothing. It will accomplish nothing. Fleshly attempts to work up the congregation will produce flesh. It will be as nothing – worthless. What is of the Holy Spirit is life-giving. The amazing thing is that allowing God to move by the Spirit through the people, always results in life. It is never in chaos. The Holy Spirit always does things in an orderly way. Anyone who has been in Spirit lead services knows the difference between a regular church service and a Holy Spirit lead service.

The point is that we go with the promptings of the Holy Spirit. There are special seasons of refreshing what God sends to refresh and build up and encourage His people. Praying for revival means allowing God to conduct the services through us. I've been apart of churches in revival, as well as churches in seasons of refreshing. During those special moves of God, missionaries are called, people rededicate their lives to

Christ. Visitors get saved. People receive healing or miracles. Lives are eternally changed by God Himself.

EZ 47: [9]Swarms of living creatures will live wherever the river flows. There will be large numbers of fish, because this water flows there and makes the salt water fresh; so where the river flows everything will live. [10]Fishermen will stand along the shore; from En Gedi to En Eglaim there will be places for spreading nets. The fish will be of many kinds—like the fish of the Mediterranean Sea.

[12]Fruit trees of all kinds will grow on both banks of the river. Their leaves will not wither, nor will their fruit fail. Every month they will bear fruit, because the water from the sanctuary flows to them. Their fruit will serve for food and their leaves for healing."

Chapter 11 Study Questions

1. Describe the aspects of the Holy Spirit that impact your life the most. Describe your relationship with Him.
2. Do you know the presence of the anointing of God on you as you minister compared to ministering by faith in the Word of God? Explain the difference. Give a specific reference.
3. Describe your prayer life and your relationship with God. What things are you doing consistently,

and what things could you add in to enrich your relationship with God?

4. Describe the most precious or special memories you have with others worshipping, praising God and or praying and studying God's Word. List at least 1 large group meeting and at least 1 small group meeting.

12 THE WORD OF GOD AT ANTIOCH

The Church at Antioch had the quality of the Word of God. They had the Torah and teachings of the Jews. They also had letters from The Apostles. That is how they preached their sermons. We today have both the Old Testament and the New testament complete. The Holy Scriptures must be an essential part of a growing church. The Word of God is the foundation of the Church. The Word of God is God's will for us. Reading it and preaching it and thinking about it brings a release of life. There is life in God's Word. The Scriptures were inspired by the Holy Spirit.

2 Peter 1: [20] Above all, you must understand that no prophecy of Scripture came about by the prophet's own interpretation of things. [21] For prophecy never had its origin in the human will, but prophets, though human, spoke from God as they were carried along by the Holy Spirit.

Simply the reading of the Word of God can bring life as it is read, people can receive spiritual nourishment from it. As it is taught by the ministry team who pray over their sermons and believe God will use them, it produces fruit in the hearts of the people. God's Word is a manual for all aspects of human life. God's word directs us, gives us instructions, education, correction etc. The Word of God must always be the plumb line. A carpenter uses a plumb line instrument to assure the walls are straight and align with the floor. The Word of God is both the foundation of what Christians believe as well as the measurement by which we measure all things. God will never violate His Word. Being led by the Holy Spirit, will never contradict God's Word – the truth of God's Word is essential to a vibrant church.

The Word of God – Hebrews 4: [12] For the word of God is alive and active. Sharper than any double-edged sword, it penetrates even to dividing soul and spirit, joints and marrow; it judges the thoughts and attitudes of the heart.

Those who become new Christians must be in a place that teaches the core truths of our Christian faith. A praying minister will always speak a Word of preach a sermon that appeals to all levels of people. God inspires the minister to preach. He or she may use an example or a scripture beyond what he or she had planned, yet it is exactly what someone in the congregation needed to hear. Spiritual milk is necessary connected to salvation and becoming a new creature in Christ. New Christians must get it, and more mature Christians who receive it only get a deeper revelation of it.

1 Peter 2: ² Like newborn babies, crave pure spiritual milk, so that by it you may grow up in your salvation, ³ now that you have tasted that the Lord is good.

Mature Christians require some teaching on what to do with what you've got. They should be equipped to teach others. The emphasis will be on applying God's Word to our lives not simply hearing it but living it and passing it on to others. Jesus spoke this word to his disciples as he evangelised a woman from Samaria. The disciples didn't know why he bothered to speak to her at all, but Jesus was evangelizing, and that one woman ran throughout her town shouting what Jesus had done for her. She was preaching Jesus. She was one of the first woman evangelists. Jesus was telling his disciples that it is necessary to preach the gospel always. There are so many people who do not yet know Christ. If you do not know what you should be doing, please evangelize or pray for God to send evangelists to share the gospel.

John 4: ⁴ "My food," said Jesus, "is to do the will of him who sent me and to finish his work. ³⁵ Don't you have a saying, 'It's still four months until harvest'? I tell you, open your eyes and look at the fields! They are ripe for harvest.

God's Word is given as an intimate life changing Word. As water cleanses, so does God's Word. God's

Word is pure and holy. As we apply it to our lives it brings cleansing.

Ephesians 5: 25 Husbands, love your wives, just as Christ loved the church and gave himself up for her 26 to make her holy, cleansing[b] her by the washing with water through the word, 27 and to present her to himself as a radiant church, without stain or wrinkle or any other blemish, but holy and blameless.

The Bereans

It is noteworthy that the Apostle mentions the Bereans because he complimented them tremendously. They did not simply believe everything the Apostles taught without searching the scriptures themselves to see it was true. They would read the scriptures and realize what the Apostles were teaching was true, so it was a confirmation of God's word by His Apostles. As we read the scriptures ourselves, God's Word appears to us directly. We should always as the Bereans read the scripture as well as receive preaching and teaching.

Acts 17: 11 Now the Berean Jews were of more noble character than those in Thessalonica, for they received the message with great eagerness and examined the Scriptures every day to see if what Paul said was true. 12 As a result, many of them believed, as did also a number of prominent Greek women and many Greek men.

Those who preach the Word

A minster of God's word must be living a life beyond reproach. That means he or she should be in willful sinning. The person should be consecrated or devoted to God. The minister or person presenting the teaching of God's Word must pray, be led by the Holy Spirit and compare the scriptures to the scriptures. The scriptures themselves prove themselves. Often, more than once, the same truth is spoken in scripture. The Word of God confirms the Word. Some things only appear once, and they are to be read within the context of the passage. For instance, a person cannot take a scripture such as "Jesus wept" and preach that we should always cry. It is ridiculous, but a mature saint would never do it. The person would be taught in the covenants, the sacraments and the Church.

2 Timothy 2: 15 Do your best to present yourself to God as one approved, a worker who does not need to be ashamed and who correctly handles the word of truth.

God gives a special command to pastors or elders who do the preaching in a church. It is a special word of encouragement. It also shows how he or she is to live with the hope of a crown of glory – a spiritual reward given by Christ.

1 Peter 5: ²Be shepherds of God's flock that is under your care, watching over them—not because you must, but because you are willing, as God wants you to be; not pursuing dishonest gain, but eager to serve; ³not lording it over those entrusted to you, but being examples to the flock. ⁴And when the Chief Shepherd appears, you will receive the crown of glory that will never fade away.

Jesus sets the example of the ultimate pastor or shepherd. He died for us. He was willing to guard us, save us with His life. A pastor must have sincere love and care for the congregation. It is a supernatural deep love that comes from Christ Himself towards the people so that all the people receive the best possible care.

A true pastor will obey the promptings of the Holy Spirit. I've known of pastors who will feel a special prompting to visit the widows and shut ins themselves sometimes. They also may pray for someone during their day. They may contact someone on their heart. The pastor protects the sheep by praying for them and encouraging them. One of my pastors would phone his people if they missed more than one service to know if they were okay. He wasn't dominating. He sincerely cared for the well being of his congregation.

John 10: [11] "I am the good shepherd. The good shepherd lays down his life for the sheep. [14] "I am the good shepherd; I know my sheep and my sheep know me— [16] I have other sheep that are not of this sheep pen. I must bring them also. They too will listen to my voice, and there shall be one flock and one shepherd.

Preaching to encourage maturity

Pastors should also preach encouraging the church to live the word of God not simply to hear it. Living the Word of God means the Word of God becomes a living part of you. The Apostle James was especially used to preach maturity. The word of God is "engrafted" (KJV) or planted within you. It means God's Word becomes so much a part of you that all of your life choices align with it. It means you speak it, but you also live it; you preach it, but you also do it.

James 1: [19] My dear brothers and sisters, take note of this: Everyone should be quick to listen, slow to speak and slow to become angry, [20] because human anger does not produce the righteousness that God desires. [21] Therefore, get rid of all moral filth and the evil that is so prevalent and humbly accept the word planted in you, which can save you.

115

The evidence of true shepherds is the sheep. The maturity of the believers in the church is an indicator of the type of pastor the church has. The Apostle Paul spoke of this as the congregation being living epistles written in our hearts. Those who receive Christ's preaching and teaching allow God's Word to come into their heart as the standard for which they will live their lives.

2 Corinthians 3: [2] You yourselves are our letter, written on our hearts, known and read by everyone. [3] You show that you are a letter from Christ, the result of our ministry, written not with ink but with the Spirit of the living God, not on tablets of stone but on tablets of human hearts.

Receiving the Word

Hearing the Word of God but not allowing it to change your life is a symptom of a hard heart or a sinful condition. Once scripture is preached, the word of God must come into your heart and you must choose to obey it. It is human will. A Christian surrenders his human will to God's Word – to God's rule. Christians should respond to the preached Word with gladness. Receiving God's Word is a joy because it causes the receiver to realize a truth of scripture. The response is joy and gratitude. It is as though you are in a restaurant and the waitress had brought you your dinner – a huge steak with potato and a salad and a cool drink. I give that comparison because it is appealing to me. You picture your favourite meal being served to you. You receive gladly. You take it to yourself. You receive as your own, so must the Word of God be with us. We must willfully receive it into our hearts, so it can be mixed with faith and produce in our lives spiritual fruit.

James 1: [22] Do not merely listen to the word, and so deceive yourselves. Do what it says. [23] Anyone who listens to the word but does not do what it says is like someone who looks at his face in a mirror [24] and, after looking at himself, goes away and immediately forgets what he looks like. [25] But whoever looks intently into the perfect law that gives freedom, and continues in it—not forgetting what they have heard, but doing it—they will be blessed in what they do.

Chapter 12 Study Questions

1. What is your favourite book in the Old Testament? Describe why.
2. What is your favourite book in the New Testament? Describe why.
3. Describe how you can integrate both the Old Covenant and New covenant into your current ministry and your future goal of ministry.

13 THE QUALITIES OF A CHRISTIAN LEADER

Spiritual maturity is not measured by spiritual gifts but by the fruit of the Spirit and the fruit of a godly life. A teacher of God's Word must live a holy life. That means he or she is not willfully sinning. He or she is not practising sin (the willful disregarding of the commandments of God). The ministers are not casual about their faith. They are set apart for God wholly. They have embraced the scriptures as their own life choices. Those who teach God's Word are held to a higher standard by God Himself and must give account as a steward would, for what he or she has done with his gifts and talents and the people and spheres of impact the person has.

1 Thessalonians 5: 23 May God himself, the God of peace, sanctify you through and through. May your whole spirit, soul and body be kept blameless at the coming of our Lord Jesus Christ.

The qualifications of a leader are described in much depth in the New testament. A minister of the gospel's life choices should align with scripture. First, he or she should be of good reputation among the saints. The person is known as a Christian by his or her life choices including marriage, alcohol use, also, personality. The pitfalls for a leader are the opposite of what is taught as spiritual guidelines for choosing a church leader. It encompasses all aspects of his or her life. It includes his personal life as well as public life, his church life, his family. All leaders in the church are held to a higher standard of living. A standard is a measurement. The measurement of what God expects from those who lead in the church are strict. The reason is that many people will know the person by his or her role in the church. The conduct of a leader should be so that others would wan to emulate that pastor or leader. As The Apostle Paul stated follow me as I follow Christ (1 Cor. 11: 1). A leader should set an example to the congregation and in all aspects of his or her life.

CHURCH LEADERS

Pastors

1 Timothy 3:1 Here is a trustworthy saying: Whoever aspires to be an overseer desires a noble task. [2] Now the overseer is to be above reproach, faithful to his wife, temperate, self-controlled, respectable, hospitable, able to teach, [3] not given to drunkenness, not violent but gentle, not quarrelsome, not a lover of money. [4] He must manage his own family well and see that his children obey him, and he must do so in a manner worthy of full[a] respect. [5] (If anyone does not know how to manage his own family, how can he take care of God's church?) [6] He must not be a recent convert, or he may become conceited and fall under the same

judgment as the devil. [7]He must also have a good reputation with outsiders, so that he will not fall into disgrace and into the devil's trap.

All leaders in the church are held to strict standards by God. Deacons or servants are also described. They usually don't preach the main sermons but have a place of serving and teaching within the church.

1 Timothy 3: [8]In the same way, deacons[b] are to be worthy of respect, sincere, not indulging in much wine, and not pursuing dishonest gain. [9]They must keep hold of the deep truths of the faith with a clear conscience. [10]They must first be tested; and then if there is nothing against them, let them serve as deacons.

[12]A deacon must be faithful to his wife and must manage his children and his household well. [13]Those who have served well gain an excellent standing and great assurance in their faith in Christ Jesus.

The Apostle Paul discipled Timothy from a youth and imparted to him his very heart. He commissioned him to oversee a church. Although Timothy was young when he was commissioned to preach, he was not a novice – he was not new to the Christian faith. He had been discipled by Paul and was with him on missionary trips. Paul encourages him not to let anyone insult him because of his youth. He instructs him in things concerning the practical aspects of church life. He reminds him to "stir up the gift' within him. The Apostle had commissioned him with prayer and prophesy.

1 Timothy 4: [11] Command and teach these things. [12] Don't let anyone look down on you because you are young, but set an example for the believers in speech, in conduct, in love, in faith and in purity. [13] Until I come, devote yourself to the public reading of Scripture, to preaching and to teaching. [14] Do not neglect your gift, which was given you through prophecy when the body of elders laid their hands on you.

[15] Be diligent in these matters; give yourself wholly to them, so that everyone may see your progress. [16] Watch your life and doctrine closely. Persevere in them, because if you do, you will save both yourself and your hearers.

Because elders or leaders in the church are held to a higher standard, they are also to be respected by the church. The scripture says double honour to those who preach the word. They are to be well paid for their service. They are not to be spoken against unless there are 2 or 3 witnesses. We should never gossip but especially regarding our leaders.

1 Timothy 5: [17] The elders who direct the affairs of the church well are worthy of double honor, especially those whose work is preaching and teaching. [18] For

Scripture says, "Do not muzzle an ox while it is treading out the grain,"[a] and "The worker deserves his wages."[b] [19] Do not entertain an accusation against an elder unless it is brought by two or three witnesses. [20] But those elders who are sinning you are to reprove before everyone, so that the others may take warning. [21] I charge you, in the sight of God and Christ Jesus and the elect angels, to keep these instructions without partiality, and to do nothing out of favoritism.

1 Corinthians 9: [11] If we have sown spiritual seed among you, is it too much if we reap a material harvest from you? [12] If others have this right of support from you, shouldn't we have it all the more?

Chapter 13 Study Questions
1. List important Church leaders who have impacted your life. List at least 1 pastor. 1 elder 1 deacon 1 Sunday School teacher. Give a brief summary for each.
2. List all areas of Church leadership you have been involved in. Describe your role for each as well as your duties and responsibilities.

14 THE CHURCH

Jesus Christ is coming back as he promised he would do. There are those who believe that Jesus will come before the judgements on the earth. They are the pre-tribulations. There are some who believe he will return in the midst of the tribulation; they are the mid-tribulations. There are some who believe the church will go through the tribulation on earth along with all the unbelievers. Since throughout the scriptures, God has never let the believers suffer judgement with unbelievers, I am a believer in the rapture of the Church or the catching up of the Church before the judgements on the unbelievers. Without going more in depth on any of these viewpoints, the truth I am asserting here is that all Christians believe Jesus Christ is coming back.

John 14: ³And if I go and prepare a place for you, I will come back and take you to be with me that you also may be where I am. ⁴You know the way to the place where I am going."

After Jesus was resurrected and had preached and appeared on the earth with the disciples for 40 days, he visibly ascended into heaven before over 500 witnesses. Angels filled the skies and spoke to the disciples of Jesus return.

Acts 1: [9]After he said this, he was taken up before their very eyes, and a cloud hid him from their sight.

[10]They were looking intently up into the sky as he was going, when suddenly two men dressed in white stood beside them. [11]"Men of Galilee," they said, "why do you stand here looking into the sky? This same Jesus, who has been taken from you into heaven, will come back in the same way you have seen him go into heaven."

Jesus with visibly descend from heaven. Many people believe this will be after the tribulation and the judgements of people on the earth. He will come riding on a white horse in glory and majesty of the King of Kings (Revelation 19: 16). We who are Christians will live with him reigning on the earth; He will dwell in the rebuilt Temple at Jerusalem. The earth will know 1000 years of peace and prosperity. This is the first resurrection. Ultimately, there will be a final war against Satan and the demons and the army of God. Then there will be a new heaven and a new earth where we will dwell for eternity.

Revelation 20: [6]Blessed and holy are those who share in the first resurrection. The second death has no power over them, but they will be priests of God and of Christ and will reign with him for a thousand years.

In Revelation 21, the Church is described as to the Bride of Christ. The beauty of the Church is as "The glorious church without spot or wrinkle or blemish" (Ephesians 5: 27). The scripture describes the Church as a Bride who has made herself ready (Rev 19:7). This means more than simply outward adornment but includes all of the Church on earth praying, fasting, giving, serving, obeying, living in the Spirit and living for God's glory, being led by the Holy Spirit etc.

The Church on earth is God's kingdom on earth. We bring the kingdom with us as individuals and we live in the kingdom of God. Although we are on the earth, we are not of the earth – we are of the new Jerusalem. Our citizenship is our destiny. We are manifesting the kingdom of God as we live on the earth. Praying, worshipping, preaching, evangelizing, giving, serving etc. are all aspects of the kingdom. Our corporate churches should resemble the indwelling of a resurrected Christ dwelling in the midst of us. Our churches should be a gathering place where heaven and earth come together with God's manifest glory. The Holy Spirit should be present as we gather together.

The Thriving Church

A thriving church is growing. Because the church is evangelizing and involved in missions as well as training its own people, the church is increasing. It is strong within because it supports itself, all members building up and strengthening each other. All parts of the body helping the other parts of the body to function. It is a place Christians desire to go and stay. It is a place of life and new life and is always full of people coming and going and attending all types of services, meetings and activities. It is of a good reputation because of the good works in the community such as feeding the hungry or stocking the shelves of the food bank.

A successful church has more than enough finances because people tithe and give above the tithe. Teaching on tithing is part of the church but also – spiritual nourishment from the services and classes releases giving in the people. A church that is not growing is symptomatic of something that should be changed. An organism grows. As the human body is constantly replenishing itself with new cells, blood circulation, growth of hair, nails etc. the church must keep living.

Humans create organizations, clubs, gathering places; they can become stagnant. Jesus will build his Church, and nothing can prevail against it (Matt 16:18). The only way is the way of obeying the Holy Spirit. Should pastors and leaders be obeying the Holy Spirit, the Church will grow. There will be manifestations of Spiritual gifts in the Church and Evangelism, salvations, healings, miracles etc. It will be a place people will get to because they know someone can pray with them of for them and their lives can be changed.

Ephesians 5: [25] Husbands, love your wives, just as Christ loved the church and gave himself up for her [26] to make her holy, cleansing[b] her by the washing with water through the word, [27] and to present her to himself as a radiant church, without stain or wrinkle or any other blemish, but holy and blameless.

The Word of God preached is as the washing of the Church. The Word of God preached feeds the people because it is more than words; it is inspired. It is not ritual – although there may be some things that are done over and over such as water baptism. Nothing in the Church is ever just a symbol. It is always meaningful. There is a Spiritual dimension to living in the Church. Although people may gather for activities such as baking or sports or any other reason, Christ is the difference. Jesus Christ is honoured in all gatherings.

The Church is a place where all people get together benefitting equally as they give to each other and receive from each other. God's presence compels the members to love each other and to provide for each other, to share with each other. Generosity, giving, serving, showing mercy, encouraging are all part of the character of the corporate churches.

Acts 2: [42] They devoted themselves to the apostles' teaching and to fellowship, to the breaking of bread and to prayer. [43] Everyone was filled with awe at the many wonders and signs performed by the apostles. [44] All the believers were together and had everything in common. [45] They sold property and possessions to give to anyone who had need. [46] Every day they continued to meet together in the temple courts. They broke bread in their homes and ate together with glad and sincere hearts, [47] praising God and enjoying the favor of all the people. And the Lord added to their number daily those who were being saved.

Small churches – large churches

There are some smaller churches and some large churches and of course mega churches. Size does not determine the character of the people – but if it is not growing, it means there is something that must be changed. Growth is a core description of a living organism. Should growth stop, the organism begins to die; without growth, soon it is no longer living.
There are Bible classes for children so that the adults can focus on the service while their children are taught scripture and are in a safe place. The Church is multicultural; there is no racial or ethnic prejudice – all people welcome. The nations of the earth will bring

glory to it (Revelation 21: 26). Translation is available for those of different languages.

Acts 2: [9] Parthians, Medes and Elamites; residents of Mesopotamia, Judea and Cappadocia, Pontus and Asia,[b] [10] Phrygia and Pamphylia, Egypt and the parts of Libya near Cyrene; visitors from Rome[11] (both Jews and converts to Judaism); Cretans and Arabs—we hear them declaring the wonders of God in our own tongues!

Essential to spiritual nourishment of a church

The pastors and leaders teach and revisit core teachings of the church yearly or regularly so that the essential doctrines of Christ as well as the covenants and study of the Old Testament are taught. Just as a person should have a steady nutritious diet, a Christian should get some of all of the Scriptures each week. The Old Testament reveals prophecies that only Jesus could fulfill so both are necessary. Building a church only on the New Testament is not balanced. Without the Torah, the prophets and other books of the Old Covenant could never have Jesus as our Saviour.

The teaching of the God of Covenant is necessary because many people in our North American, Western society do not understand the meaning of Covenant. It is an Eastern tradition and necessary for all to understand or we cannot comprehend the New Covenant of Jesus Christ or his precious blood. The Covenants God made with people should be studied and revisited as those truths apply to our lives as well: Adam, Noah, Abraham, Moses, New Covenant through Jesus Christ.

The Sacraments are not only for the denominational churches. They were taught or modelled by Jesus and should be taught and practiced by the corporate Church. Sacraments include marriage, baby dedication, confirmation, communion, anointing with oil, baptisms, foot washing, laying on of hands with prophesy. There are some charismatic and Pentecostal churches who no longer practice all of them. There are some denominational churches that do not practice all of them. The Church must keep these things quick because they are not simply traditions of men but brought to us from Christ.

Teaching of Church Doctrine

Pastors and leaders should teach doctrine, covenants, sacraments, Christian life, Bible studies. It should not only be taught once but repeated just as a person doesn't eat a steak once and never again. Biblical truths should be taught and revisited – not restated but revisited with prayer and Holy Spirit inspiration. The truths should be living in us so that should someone ask us what we believe, we could talk and talk and talk of the things the Scriptures teach.

Doctrine – Hebrews 6:1 Therefore let us move beyond the elementary teachings about Christ and be taken forward to maturity, not laying again the foundation of repentance from acts that lead to death,[a] and of faith in God,[2] instruction about cleansing rites,[b] the laying on of hands, the resurrection of the dead, and eternal judgment. [3] And God permitting, we will do so.

Ministry Gifts

All the five-fold ministry gifts are functioning in the Church. Pastors and leaders know their callings and bring in others who've got other callings so that the Church is always receiving impartations from the ministry. Apostles are calling forth and imparting gifts, developing, mentoring, discipling, releasing and commissioning people – to plant churches and go on missions etc. It's done publicly in the services so that all the sheep can see the ministry gifts flowing in the Church.

Prophets are encouraging, exhorting comforting in the services and small groups as well as some prophets – recognizing gifts, calling gifts, imparting gifts, commissioning (along with Apostles) the saints who are going on missionary trips, evangelizing or planting churches.

Evangelists are preaching salvation, healing, deliverance, Biblical prosperity - giving. People know if they bring loved ones to church there will be an altar call and there will be healings and miracles. The gift of faith is in the Church.

Praise and worship are not just singing songs. It is a lavishing of love onto God as the woman with the alabaster box who poured the precious ointment within it onto Jesus (Matt. 26: 7-). There may be prophetic worship – tongues interpretation during the worship – liberty. It is not the same song we sing twice because as we worship there is new inspiration and declaration of passion for God.

There may be worshipping in tongues and in English, prophetic praise, spontaneous praise and silence where we all bow on our knees in reverence. Some may lie prostrate on the ground in silence. Altar calls might come at the start of a service or during or at the end – leaders are led by the Holy Spirit, obeying the promptings of the Holy Spirit.

The leaders leading the church in life in the Spirit

The pastors and the leaders are dancing, clapping, singing, worshipping and setting an example for the church by their worship as well as their lives.

Galatians 5: [25] Since we live by the Spirit, let us keep in step with the Spirit.

Galatians 5: [22] But the fruit of the Spirit is love, joy, peace, forbearance, kindness, goodness, faithfulness, [23] gentleness and self-control. Against such things there is no law.

Romans 8: [14] For those who are led by the Spirit of God are the children of God.

Chapter 14 Study Questions

1. Create a list of at least 20 main topics you believe must be taught more than once in a local church.
2. Describe how a Church can both teach doctrine and flow in the Holy Spirit. Have you been a part of a local church that has? Describe it.
3. Write a story of how God has used you by the promptings of the Holy Spirit to minister to someone or a group.
4. Did you commit all yourself to God as in 1 Thess. 5: 23 spirit, soul, body? If not – please do it.

15 THE IMPORTANCE OF THE ALTAR

Most of our charismatic and Pentecostal churches, the altar is a place on the floor in front of the platform. People gather there to pray. It is more than a place to pray – it is a place of life and death. It is a place of dying to self and saying yes to Christ. It is a place of destiny decisions and we should not make it less important. We should emphasize it in each service. It is not a place you go to once and never again. All the sheep should be making an altar at the altar each week. It is a place where the Word of God is confirmed in us and impartations are received. There are altar prayer workers who can pray with people or people can pray alone. It is a place where the sinner is saved, and the saints present themselves fresh to God.

Abraham met God and established an altar. He built it. He consecrated himself and received from God the words God spoke to him. He did it more than once. Each occasion God spoke to him, Abraham built a new altar. It was a place of accepting and submitting to what God had spoken. Each of these instances marked a change in his life.

Abraham Genesis 12: [8] From there he went on toward the hills east of Bethel and pitched his tent, with Bethel on the west and Ai on the east. There he built

an altar to the LORD and called on the name of
the LORD.

Abraham Genesis 13: [18] So Abram went to live near
the great trees of Mamre at Hebron, where he
pitched his tents. There he built an altar to the LORD.

There was a special altar where God instructed
Abraham what to do. He instructed him to sacrifice
certain animals and divide their bodies in two. It was
a place where God's Holy presence went in between
the sacrifice and consecrated it and received it. It
was a place of eternal consequence as Abrahamic
covenant was established.

Genesis 15: [17] When the sun had set and darkness
had fallen, a smoking firepot with a blazing
torch appeared and passed between the pieces. [18] On
that day the LORD made a covenant with Abram and
said, "To your descendants I give this land, from the
Wadi[c] of Egypt to the great river, the Euphrates—
[19] the land of the Kenites, Kenizzites,
Kadmonites, [20] Hittites,Perizzites, Rephaites, [21] Amorit
es, Canaanites, Girgashites and Jebusites."

Jacob built an altar after his speaking with
God. It was a destiny decision. He chose to follow
God with all his life.

Genesis 35: [14] Jacob set up a stone pillar at the place
where God had talked with him, and he poured out a
drink offering on it; he also poured oil on it. [15] Jacob

called the place where God had talked with him Bethel.[9]

Abraham built altars after God speaking with him. They were places of confirmation: receiving from God and offering a sacrifice of praise.

King David had sinned and because of it all of Israel was suffering from a plague. David begged God for a solution as he knew it was his fault and he didn't want more people to die. He went to the spot God directed him to and he built an altar there. It had consequences immediately – the plague was stopped. God received the sacrifice as an atonement.

David built an altar

1 Chronicles 21: [18] Then the angel of the LORD ordered Gad to tell David to go up and build an altar to the LORD on the threshing floor of Araunah the Jebusite.[19] So David went up in obedience to the word that Gad had spoken in the name of the LORD.

2 Samuel 24: [25] David built an altar to the LORD there and sacrificed burnt offerings and fellowship offerings. Then the LORD answered his prayer in behalf of the land, and the plague on Israel was stopped.

Moses built an altar after a tremendous defeating of the enemy. He did it to honour God giving Him glory.

Exodus 17: [15] Moses built an altar and called it
The LORD is my Banner. [16] He said, "Because hands
were lifted up against[c] the throne of
the LORD,[d] the LORD will be at war against the
Amalekites from generation to generation."

Later God established "the altar" as a necessary
part of worship of God. He instructed Moses how to
build it and gave instruction, so the priests could use it.
It was a place where the blood of animals was offered
for human sin. It could not erase the sin, but it was a
place of atonement. God accepted the sacrifice until
Jesus came and shed his blood for us to erase – all sin
and iniquity to those who believe on him (1 John 1: 7).

Judaism is not man's religion of how to serve God;
it is direct obedience to God's instructions to the
prophets. Judaism was started by God communicating
with man. The Mosaic altar was established by God. God
gave instruction on the size, shape dimensions as well as
the offerings.

Exodus 27: 1- 8   God instructed Moses on how to build
an altar for sacrifice. Sheep, rams, bulls, doves
established as sacrifices as burnt offerings.

Solomon establishes an altar at the Temple

King David desired to build a temple for God, but God wouldn't let him, so David got the plans for how to build it and gathered all the materials and finances knowing that his son Solomon would do it. The altar was necessary in the Old Testament because people couldn't approach God directly, or they would die because God is Holy and people are not. The altar was a place to offer a sin offering, or a thanksgiving offering etc.

2 Chronicles 1: . ⁵But the bronze altar that Bezalel son of Uri, the son of Hur, had made was in Gibeon in front of the tabernacle of the LORD; so Solomon and the assembly inquired of him there. ⁶Solomon went up to the bronze altar before the LORD in the tent of meeting and offered a thousand burnt offerings on it.

New Testament Altar

In the New testament we receive Jesus shed blood at Calvary for our sins. We receive it once and we become Christians. Should we sin, we make an altar quickly: we repent, accept Jesus shed blood and accept forgiveness of sins. There are many opportunities for such altars. They are destiny decision places. Because Christ lives in us in the person of the Holy Spirit, we can pray constantly and in any place. We can repent, praise, worship any place we go. How much so more important is the place of the altar in our congregations. It can be gathering at the front of the church, but it can also be praying at your seat. It can be kneeling or standing. It is a spiritual posture of receiving from God. It is a place of giving of all of oneself to God. We offer ourselves as a living sacrifice to God (Romans 12: 1-2).

Hebrews 9: ¹⁴How much more, then, will the blood of Christ, who through the eternal Spirit offered himself unblemished to God, cleanse our consciences from acts that lead to death,⁽ᶜ⁾ so that we may serve the living God!

The Significance of the Altar

The altar is a place of sacrifice. We are the sacrifice. We repent, receive blessings, receive strength, healing, promises from God etc. The preaching of the Word is received in our hearts and we are changed by our coming to the altar. It is a destiny decision place of accepting new truths and recommitting our lives. It is of most importance in our gatherings. There should always be an opportunity to honour God by going forward for prayer, praise, worship, etc.

The altar call should be specific also. There should be some place to receive the truths taught that day in the service. There should be a place of decision where the saints can step forward not only with their bodies but in their hearts move closer to God. The confirming of truths, things settled – resolved – permanence of decisions there are matters of eternity. Life changing destiny decisions are made at the altar: salvation, healing, deliverance, consecration, thanksgiving, accepting God's instructions/God's Word, marriage, baby dedication, confirmation, prayer and impartation from others, prophecy, commissioning etc.

Preaching God's Word

The Word of God should always be two-way communication: the giving of the word by the pastor or leader and the receiving of the word by the congregation. An altar call is necessary. It is the place of receiving. It can be short or long but the moving of one's body for the purpose of confirming the truth is often necessary. You could make an altar at your seat, or you could go to the front of the church. Your making of an altar is a willful decision to put God first. It is a place of consecration.

Prayer at the altar-is an outward representation of a deep spiritual inner work.

Chapter 15 Study Questions
1. Describe the role of an altar in your life. Give testimony of at least 3 occasions it changed your life.

2. Have you yourself ministered at the altar? Describe your role and the importance of the anointing, the gifts of the Holy Spirit and the study of God's Word during your ministry.
3. In your goal of ministry, how can you add in an altar aspect so those receiving always get a chance to draw closer to God?
4. Describe your daily life devotions. Is there always an altar?

16 CHURCH LIFE

Supernatural should be normal in a church. It is a dynamic gathering of God's people to worship, praise, pray, study God's Word and receive answers to prayer.

Aiming the church in the right direction starts with the pastors and leaders. Teaching, preaching, and emphasizing the core beliefs results in all the church believing the same things.

Finances

The finances of the church should be more than sufficient, so that the church can do more than maintain itself. There should be a surplus of, money so the church can evangelize, take part in missions' trips, host prayer gatherings and take part in outreach ministries in its community – some churches support their missionaries, missions' outreaches, and evangelistic efforts such as musicals, dramas, concerts, dinners etc. The response will be the growth of the church.

Evangelistic meetings

Evangelistic outreach ministries can be in the church building and, in the communities in parks or public buildings that can be booked or rented. These services should include praise, worship and preaching on salvation, healing and deliverance as well as other inspired topics. An evangelistic outreach requires faith in the word preached. That means signs and wonders should follow the preaching. The word itself is not a teaching but a preaching. The main difference is the target audience are people who may not be familiar with the Bible. Scripture should be used of course – but it is preaching. Bible studies are for Christians or those hoping to become Christians. The gift of faith is necessary in the preacher as well as the team assisting him or her.

Healing services – Acts 19: [11] God did extraordinary miracles through Paul, [12] so that even handkerchiefs and aprons that had touched him were taken to the sick, and their illnesses were cured and the evil spirits left them.

Mark 16: [15] *He said to them, "Go into all the world and preach the gospel to all creation. [16] Whoever believes and is baptized will be saved, but whoever does not believe will be condemned. [17] And these signs will accompany those who believe: In my name they will drive out demons; they will speak in new tongues; [18] they will pick up snakes with their hands; and when they drink deadly poison, it will not hurt them at all; they will place their hands on sick people, and they will get well."*

19 After the Lord Jesus had spoken to them, he was taken up into heaven and he sat at the right hand of God. 20 Then the disciples went out and preached everywhere, and the Lord worked with them and confirmed his word by the signs that accompanied it.

James 5: 15 And the prayer offered in faith will make the sick person well; the Lord will raise them up. If they have sinned, they will be forgiven.

Deliverance Ministry

There is regular teaching and preaching about living free in Christ. The people know that God desires for us to be free from bondage. Deliverance from addictions, sinful habits and demonic influence should be practised in the Church. Evangelistic services will often combined with healing, anointing with oil, deliverance.

Apostles, Prophets and Evangelists flow in deliverance ministry but it can be done by any believing Christian. How much more should it be present in our churches as important. The Apostle Paul practised it as did Jesus. We were commanded to set the captives free. The only way this can occur is that we commit ourselves to do it in our services. If new pastors don't know how to conduct deliverance ministry– they should be trained so they can learn how. The only way to learn is by assisting a mature Christian believer who practices it. It is a what I would term a two- step program: cast the demons out and let the person consecrate himself to God.

Acts 16: [16] Once when we were going to the place of prayer, we were met by a female slave who had a spirit by which she predicted the future. She earned a great deal of money for her owners by fortune-telling. [17] She followed Paul and the rest of us, shouting, "These men are servants of the Most High God, who are telling you the way to be saved." [18] She kept this up for many days. Finally, Paul became so annoyed that he turned around and said to the spirit, "In the name of Jesus Christ I command you to come out of her!" At that moment the spirit left her.

After the demon is cast out, it is necessary the person consecrate himself wholly to God. The word of God must take root in his heart so he can remain free.

Romans 12:1 Therefore, I urge you, brothers and sisters, in view of God's mercy, to offer your bodies as a living sacrifice, holy and pleasing to God—this is your true and proper worship. [2] Do not conform to the pattern of this world, but be transformed by the renewing of your mind. Then you will be able to test and approve what God's will is—his good, pleasing and perfect will.

1 Thessalonians 5: [23] May God himself, the God of peace, sanctify you through and through. May your

whole spirit, soul and body be kept blameless at the coming of our Lord Jesus Christ.

Prayer Teams

At the altars, there should be the most important type of ministry of praying with people. It is a place of encouragement – prophesy – impartation and blessing. The pastors should be there as well as those trained to pray with people.

Ephesians 4: [11] So Christ himself gave the apostles, the prophets, the evangelists, the pastors and teachers, [12] to equip his people for works of service, so that the body of Christ may be built up [13] until we all reach unity in the faith and in the knowledge of the Son of God and become mature, attaining to the whole measure of the fullness of Christ.

There should be praying over those who come to the altar and to the church receiving new members there as well as praying over those who leave – whether they are leaving to a different church or moving. It is a place we can impart a blessing. There will be no wounded sheep or pastors should we pray over those coming or leaving the church. It's also a spiritual protection and transference of it.

The importance of the local church

The regular aspects of church life should be of vital importance to a Christian's life. It is a place of gathering for services but also the regular teachings and functions of a local church: sacraments, covenants, teaching preaching, prayer, praise, gifts of the Spirit, marriages, funerals, baby dedications, and other celebrations.

There should be special conferences and celebrations, with some services dedicated to the release, stirring up and impartation of gifts of the Spirit.

These special aspects describe a thriving local church:

The centre of the social community of the believers. There are Bible classes for people of all ages. There are regular scheduled services. There are children and youth activities. There is Prayer service. There are special Bible classes – taught by others not only the pastor.

There are special church celebrations and conferences or special gatherings for prayer, praise, worship, preaching, ministry, etc. with refreshments.

There are activities such as sports or music for all ages: children, youth, and adults. There are special evangelistic corporate church efforts such as concerts, dramas, bake sales, and special speakers.

There are small groups or cell groups in large churches so that everyone can use his or her spiritual gifts – special Bible study, praise and prayer. Everyone has a spiritual covering. The pastor gets reports from the elders, deacons or cell group leaders regularly on any important issues.

The pastors are approachable in small or large churches. There is a special bond between the sheep and their pastor. The congregation loves its pastor, but each individual also does and should have some type of relationship with the leadership. In large churches, special dinners, picnics, concerts etc. is a place for the pastor to connect with people. There could be church dinners – in some large churches, they have their own restaurant. Other smaller churches offer dinners to raise money for missions.

There is always room for new ideas and suggestions of special activities. A member should feel he or she can approach the pastor with an idea or suggestion. All members, and regular attendees, should have a place they can serve or volunteer. Serving is a way of connecting with the rest of the Body. Belonging includes body ministry and body functions. The people in the church know each other because of their involvement. It is a desired place because of the presence of God, the people, the pastors, the praise and worship, the teaching and preaching as well as the other special activities.

Chapter 16 Study Questions

1. Does your local church regularly host evangelistic meetings or outreaches? List them. Describe ones you have been a part of.
2. Explain your comfort level and experience with deliverance ministry.
3. Explain your own evangelistic giftings and experiences. Is it easy for you? List the ones you've been a part of? Is it easier in groups? Is there experience with both?

17 SPECIAL GATHERINGS

There are special gatherings in a vibrant Church. They are special celebrations during the holidays, or church conferences. They started with God instructing Moses that there should be special celebrations for Israel. God established festivals and feasts.

Leviticus 23:1 The LORD said to Moses, ²"Speak to the Israelites and say to them: 'These are my appointed festivals, the appointed festivals of the LORD, which you are to proclaim as sacred assemblies.

Jews and Messianic Jews keep the feasts of Passover, offering of first fruits, festival of weeks, festival of trumpets, Day of Atonement, the festival of tabernacles as God instructed Moses.

There were special gatherings that God ordained for the Israelites that should be kept forever. Some Christians do keep these celebrations. Some do not. The early Church kept them because they were Jews; they are commanded to keep the Mosaic covenant. As the gospel spread to the Gentiles, the Council of Jerusalem's decision that it was not necessary for Gentiles to become Jews. We are not obligated to keep them. Although not necessary to keep the Jewish holidays, I encourage believing Christians to take part in Messianic Jewish celebrations, because it will only lead to a deeper understanding of Christ.

The important aspect is there should be special gatherings of the church for shared meals, worship, praise, prayer, preaching, giving. This is not always in all churches. There should be guest preachers and teachers and missionaries. The church body should receive refreshing by the 5-fold ministry not only the main pastors of the church. It should be scheduled regularly.

God instituted the Sabbath – a day of rest. The church gathers to offer sacrifices of praise and worship as well as learn from God's Word, pray and give. The Jews celebrate the Sabbath on a Friday as the sun goes down and on the Saturday. Christians almost always celebrate it on the Sunday because Jesus rose from the dead on a Sunday. Jesus was criticized for healing people on the Sabbath. He proclaimed that he should do the will of God and that he is the Sabbath.

Matthew 12: 8 For the Son of Man is Lord of the Sabbath."

He was not eliminating the commandments; He was fulfilling them showing the will of God to save, heal, deliver etc. always. With Jesus as the LORD of the Sabbath, a person will not become religious or ritualistic without spiritual life.

The Sabbath

Leviticus 23: ³"'There are six days when you may work, but the seventh day is a day of sabbath rest, a day of sacred assembly. You are not to do any work; wherever you live, it is a sabbath to the LORD.

Team Ministry

With all the aspects of church life discussed, no one pastor can do it all. A team of pastors in large churches, allows for some ministers to specialize in different areas such as evangelism or teaching doctrine etc. Also, elders and deacons must be established. They are necessary for the functioning of a church. They can assist in the sacraments and in visitation and outreach. The congregation will respond with serving and the ministry of helps as they are presented with opportunities.

Connecting the Body of Christ as well as evangelizing

There should be meetings with all ages present together in praise, prayer, worship, preaching. There should be some interaction with all ages of the church with each other. These - all church services - could be periodically, but they are essential so that all the church know each other.

There should be regular evangelizing efforts by all ages of the church. Rather than only a church men's dinner, invite a friend dinner. This could include children (Sunday school or VBS) and teens. It should be periodically and purposefully.

Chapter 17 Study Questions
1. What special gatherings does your local church take part in?
2. What gatherings have you been a part of with other churches or through Christian media?
3. Write a description of the atmosphere of a large corporate Church gathering. Explain your conviction of the importance of it.

18 CHRISTIAN BROADCASTING: THE DIGITAL CHURCH

Christian broadcasting and media connect believers throughout the earth. It offers preaching, teaching, evangelism, worship, praise, concerts, movies, dramas, streaming from churches live, documentaries, talk shows, world news from a Christian perspective, offer channels especially for teens, children as well as adults. There is often translation or separate language stations for global coverage.

Christian media is especially important for shut ins, singles, elderly, pioneer Christians, or connection to others of the same faith. Talk shows host worship, praise, preaching, teaching, and Christians from all areas of life – business, writers, media, arts, etc. Movies, dramas, documentaries, special concerts, church services, Christian ministries preaching, teaching, for children, teens, adults, Christian world news – from a Biblical perspective, Christian world news with prophetic interpretations, makes the Christian channels always interesting.

It is an excellent resource for all types of Christians. It is a vital line of communion with the Body of Christ global.

On line Church

It cannot replace a person's belonging in a group of believers in a local church fully. It often is a place people turn to who cannot get to church or who are not in a local church or between churches and some church is best rather than none. The members of the body of Christ are to communicate with each other – body ministry – prayer for each other as well as the gifts of the spiritual being used. I don't know of any digital church that has this ability.

Christian Media

Many Christians are encouraged and built up by the following:

Christian Radio and TV - music, praise, worship, inspiration talking, commercials from Christian businesses, preaching, announcements for Christian events – It is a life-line for those who are the only Christian in their families.

Christian magazines - News articles, Inspirational articles, reviews of new releases of Christian media, global perspective on Christian and news events are featured.

To those who are shut ins – There is a direct connection with the Body of Christ global. Some churches are formally all digital with membership on line. Most large churches are streaming services and special events. Some churches post podcasts.

Chapter 18 Study Questions
1. Do you regularly use Christian media? Explain each and its importance in your life.
2. Give a testimony of how Christian tv, radio, print has changed your life or impacted you.
3. Do you believe that Christian media can replace the local church. Explain why.
4. Did you experience the release of the gifts of the Spirit during Christian media. What did you do? Describe it in comparison to the anointing during a regular church service or Christian gathering.

CONCLUSION

Throughout this book, main aspects of the Charismatic Church were presented. Qualities of an excellent living Church, and the things that make it thrive are written.

As a pastor or Church leader or student of Christian ministry, hopefully you have recognized some of the traits of an effective church and have considered them regarding your own ministry.

It is my prayer that you will relate to some of the aspects of the Charismatic Church, become aware of the truths of Scripture you have not considered and integrate the things you can use in your ministry.

Only through the joining together of Apostles, Prophets, Pastors, Teachers and Evangelists can we together build up and encourage the Body of Christ. It is only by the equipping of the saints that the kingdom of God will be preached throughout all the earth.

Should each minister or student of ministry consider the important dimensions of the Church (covered in this book, and of course others yet to be discussed), there will be a yearning for Spiritual revival and a quickening of people that will stir them to preach and teach these truths to others within their spheres of influence. This is my ultimate reason for writing the book – to quicken, to inspire, to begin intercessory prayer concerning these things that there may be Spiritual Revival in the Church so that the glory of Christ in the Church will be revealed.

PRAYERS

PRAYERS

The following prayers are samples of prayers you could pray for important reasons. You could pray the same meaning in your own words. The prayers are meant as examples only.

PRAYER FOR SALVATION

Thank you- Jesus that you died for me on the cross. Thank you that you rose from the dead and ascended into heaven. Thank you that you are coming back again. I thank you Jesus for forgiving my sins. Thank you for your blood that cleanses me from all sin and unrighteousness. Thank you that your blood makes me holy. Thank you for saving me. Fill me with the Holy Spirit to overflowing. I pray for the baptism of the Holy Spirit. Lead me to other people who love you and serve you and that can help me know more about you. Give me the discerning of spirits strong. I thank you and praise you. With my mouth, I confess Jesus Christ is my LORD. Amen.

PRAYER FOR BAPTISM OF THE HOLY SPIRIT

Thank you- Jesus that you promised to send the gift of the Holy Spirit to us. Thank you that this promise is to all believers. I am a believer. I want all of you that you will give me. I want to know you God. Baptize me in the Holy Spirit with the evidence of speaking in other tongues. I believe you want to fill me to overflowing with your Spirit so that I might be an effective witness for Christ on the earth. Thank you for saving me. Thank you for your Holy presence. [begin praising God for what He has done for you – sing worship choruses and praise God in your natural language. Believe that He is present with you – start praising and worshipping Him. As phrases come to you in other tongues, say them – praise God with new tongues.] I praise you. I thank you. I receive the baptism of the Holy Spirit.

PRAYER FOR RELEASING ANGELS

God, I thank you that angels are ministering spirits sent as ministers to us. I pray over my prayer request NAME IT HERE. God I pray release angels to perform it. I thank you for releasing the answer to me. I praise you for it. Amen.

PRAYER FOR RESISTING EVIL

I am the redeemed of the LORD. Jesus Christ has saved me. I am a new creation in Christ Jesus. Jesus blood covers me. I live in the spirit. The Holy Spirit of God fills my spirit. O Holy Spirit quicken me; give me wisdom. Pray [expecting God will give you discerning of spirits so you will have the right words to speak.]

In the name of Jesus Christ, I bind you. I rebuke you evil spirit. In the name of Jesus, I command you to go out. You have no place in my life. I cast you out. You have no place with me. I am covered by the blood of Jesus and His righteousness is my righteousness. Go out evil spirit in the name of Jesus Christ!

Thank you, Holy Spirit for your holy presence. Release angels to drive out the enemy. Thank you. Amen.

PRAYER FOR PROTECTION

Holy Spirit release angels to protect me. I plead the blood of Jesus over me. I pray the protection you promise to your people. Cover me Jesus. Holy Spirit give me wisdom, discernment and understanding. Thank you for angels that guard over me. Thank you for your blood that protects me and a hedge of protection around me. I praise you O God. [praise God with some worship choruses and expect God's holy presence to be manifest in you]. Thank you. O God for protection.

PRAYER FOR HEALING

Lord Jesus, thank you that you gave your life for me so that I can be saved, healed and delivered. I thank you for the scripture that by your stripes I am healed. I thank you for my healing.

NAME THE DISEASE I bind you in the name of Jesus. I cast you out. I pray over myself that I would be whole spirit, soul and body.

Thank you, God. for your healing manifestation in my life. I give you all the glory. Amen.

PRAYER OF REPENTENCE

Jesus, thank you for your blood shed for me. I repent of the sin of NAME IT. I thank you for liberty from sin. I cut off the root of iniquity in my family. I thank you for your empowering presence to live a Holy life. Holy Spirit lead and guide me in the paths of righteousness. Thank you for giving me godly desires. Let my life align with your word. In Jesus name. Amen.

Prayer of dedication as a giver

God, thank you for prospering me. Let me be a giver you can use to give to others. God let my character be humble and giving so that you place things and wealth in my hands, and I will give as you lead me. If you prosper me with more than enough, I will obey your promptings to give to the gospel, to people and for the glory of God. Use me as a giver. I give myself wholly to you. In Jesus name. Amen.

OTHER BOOKS BY
CHRIS A. LEGEBOW

Available on Amazon.ca Amazon.com or Kindle

By Living Word Publishers

Angels: Ministering Spirits

Discipling the Generation

An Excellent Spirit: Living Life Wholly Unto God

Covenant With God: God's Relationship With Man

Discovering and Using your Spiritual Gifts

Discipling The Generation

Divine Healing in the Scriptures: God's Mercy Towards Man

Jesus Christ: Saviour, Healer, Deliverer, LORD

Kinds of Giving: From the Holy Scriptures

Signs of Jesus Coming

Spheres of Authority: Know yours

The Commandments

The Doctrine of Christ: Essential Truths of Scripture

Continued…

OTHER BOOKS BY
CHRIS A. LEGEBOW

The Five-Fold Ministry: Gifts to the Church

Kinds of Prayer. Knowing Them and Using Them Effectively

Living Life Fully: Knowing your Purpose

The Anointing: the Glory of God

The High Calling: Life Worth Living

The High Life: Communion with the Holy Spirit

The Sacraments: A Charismatic Guide

ABOUT THE AUTHOR

Chris Legebow is a Christian Professor of English and Communications. She has taught at the elementary, high school and College and University levels. She has ministered in her local churches in intercessory prayer, teaching Sunday school and other Christian Doctrine classes to children and youth. She has preached to congregations and given her testimony. Although she was not raised in a Christian home, she came to know Jesus Christ as her Saviour and LORD while she was studying in University. This radically transformed her life in terms of priorities and commitment.

She has a strong passion for the great commission – that Jesus Christ would be preached throughout all the earth believing that it a major sign of the LORD's return. She has been a part of several different types of full gospel charismatic churches but has also gained much of her insight and enlightenment from Christian Media and broadcasting. She hopes to continue ministering, serving, interceding and giving and teaching until the LORD returns.

www.ingramcontent.com/pod-product-compliance
Lightning Source LLC
Chambersburg PA
CBHW032035040426
42449CB00007B/893